LESSONS FROM THE BEST

Holistic Insights, Tips, and Tricks
to Improve Your Golf

Mark Immelman
& James Sitar

Foreword by Jim Nantz

BACK NINE PRESS

Back Nine Press
Chicago, Illinois
www.back9press.com
Twitter and Instagram: @backninepress

9 8 7 6 5 4 3 2 1

First Edition
Printed in China

Library of Congress Cataloging-in-Publication Data:

ISBN 978-1-956237-20-7 (hardcover)
ISBN 978-1-956237-21-4 (e-book)

From Mark:

To my ever-loving, ever-believing,
ever-motivating, ever-patient wife and life-partner,
Tracy Martin.

You truly are heaven-sent, and words cannot express
how thankful I am to have you at my side.

You make me a better man and I love you ... forever.

From James:

To my parents, who have taught me so much.
And to Molly and Stella, the loves of my life.

CONTENTS

Mark is right guy at the right time to come in and help thousands of us with this sport we love. He has found a way to teach us, with grace and positivity, with a wide range of lessons from legendary players and teachers. All of these insightful teachings are gleaned from Mark's own curious mind.

Jim Nantz

Foreword

JIM NANTZ

cu·ri·os·i·ty
noun
   1. a strong desire to learn or know something.

Curiosity is a word that I cherish, and one that was used to describe my late father when I wrote *Always By My Side* about him years ago. My dad had a curious mind, and that was one of the many gifts he passed along to his adoring son.

I think of that word, *curiosity*, when I think of my distinguished colleague and friend, Mark Immelman. Mark has a kind and gentle way about him, while possessing an unobtrusive inquisitiveness that makes you realize he seeks answers to what makes people unique. It's a wonderful trait, really, especially the way Mark goes about it. He finds the best in everyone while engaging in a positive and intellectually stimulating way.

When Mark asked me to hit the opening tee shot for

this important book, it was something I immediately wanted to do. These days, the world can get bogged down in negative dialogue and actions. Too much polarization, too many hot takes to maintain a civilized culture. Refreshingly, that is not Mark.

He is a faith-based man with deep and meaningful relationships both personally and professionally. He has always sought the best in others. That includes, as you are about to find out, what makes golfers perform to the best of their ability.

That is why in many respects Mark is the right guy at the right time to come in and help thousands of us with this sport we love. He has found a way to teach us, with grace and positivity, with a wide range of lessons from legendary players and teachers. All of these insightful teachings are gleaned from Mark's own curious mind.

It's brilliant what he has amassed here. We all know that golf is the most difficult sport to perfect, and that there are countless ways to approach the golf swing. Finally, we can discover just how unique and individualistic a golf swing can be, and at the same time, we can find a number of ways that each and every one of us can relate to and ultimately benefit.

A confession before we embark on this enjoyable journey: I've known Mark (and his wonderful brother Trevor) for years and was struck immediately by the way he was raised. Kudos to June and Johan Immelman. They gave their kids a path to a fulfilling life—teaching them a brilliant command of the language, an undying passion for golf and its virtues, and a spirit for finding goodness in others.

I trust you will enjoy these riveting pages as you take your love of the game to whole new level. Thank you Mark for your stewardship. As always, you are *On The Mark*!

—JIM NANTZ

INTRODUCTION

Mark Immelman

I am a golf-nerd ... certifiably so. I think about the game constantly. Not necessarily *my* game; most times I'm thinking about other golfers' games.

Maybe it's my golf instructor background, or the coach inside me, or maybe it's my PGA Tour broadcaster-analyst side. Either way, if you scroll through my social media feed, or look at my bookshelf, you'll typically find books on golf.

Ever since I was introduced to the game, I was enamored with everything about it. I vividly recall my childhood days at the Somerset West Country Club (in South Africa, just southeast of Cape Town). My mother would drop me at the course, and I'd play 27 to 36 holes, and then practice or have some sort of putting or chipping competition afterward.

I couldn't get enough. I didn't know much, but I did know hard work...and reading. And in an effort to improve my game, I developed a voracious appetite for both.

Ben Hogan's *Five Lessons: The Modern Fundamentals of Golf* became my *de facto* golf bible, and I hung on every word—and sketch—in the book. While I learned a lot, I was like most golfers trying to improve their games: I was armed with lots of information and knowledge, but not very much wisdom or understanding. Who wouldn't want Hogan's swing? I blindly followed his advice. Some of it certainly helped, and some of it did not. Indeed, with the benefit of experience and hindsight, I firmly believe that I did my game a disservice by trying it.

Anyhow, thankfully there was a silver lining. The lessons I learned from that experience became a golf instruction mantra of mine: Seek understanding as you gather information and knowledge. What's the point of knowing something about the golf swing, if you can't properly apply it?

I became an accomplished golfer and a tournament winner at the amateur and collegiate level, but after that, I had limited success in the paid ranks. Perhaps that was because I only played three professional events before my money ran out. Perhaps deep down I knew that my chances of becoming the best golfer in the world were scuttled by my younger brother, Trevor. Either way, I had reached a crossroads in my golf career.

Nine years my junior, Trevor was a star in the making and was routinely beating his NCAA All-American brother. It helped to get me to a big dose of realism, and it quickly occurred to me that I was going to be a better coach and teacher than a player in the touring ranks. I took to giving lessons to friends, family, and my younger brother, and I found my groove quickly. Golf instruction afforded me the opportunity to use my inclination for teaching while being immersed in the game that I had grown to love. I'd learn from the best, and then apply my learning for their particular swings and games.

Success as an instructor came quickly. I was told that I had the communication skills and ability to make complex concepts simple and easy to digest and apply. Others have referenced my appetite for reading. Yet others have highlighted my playing experience and my ability to teach golf beyond swing techniques. Whatever it was, my stable of international clients grew, and I found myself on practice areas and ranges at professional tournaments.

I was a part of the Sony HandiCam era of golf instructors. You could see us coming: we all looked the same, with our little black bags protecting our most valuable possession: our video cameras. We were a dime a dozen. And if we were fortunate—and a little industrious—we would have footage of some of the great golf swings of our time, such as Tiger Woods, Ernie Els, and Nick Faldo. There was no YouTube, and no video tapes you could buy. You'd have to film the footage yourself, recorded on cassettes, or gather it from someone else who got it themselves.

HandiCam instructors were armed and ready to compare your swing to that of the model, and then point out where your shortcomings were. Fast forward (no pun intended), we would likely just be fixing symptomatic problems to make the swing look better, more aesthetically pleasing. Really, all we were doing was succeeding in teaching golf swings and not golfers. We were unaware that we were impressing upon people the message that they could only play well if their swings looked a certain way.

There's a *lot* more to scoring well than having a pretty swing.

And then I had a brush with Jim Furyk, and my world got rocked. I'll never forget when another golfer, watching Furyk, asked me what I would say if Furyk asked me for swing advice. It was a question that stumped me, even though I cobbled together an answer riddled with jargon and instruction-isms. That question kept me awake for many nights. The question became a watershed moment in my teaching career: I began to realize that there's more to the golf swing than a certain plane, a certain rhythm, a certain aesthetic, with common positional characteristics. I began to think more widely about how great golfers get results. This led me to approach instruction in a more holistic way.

> *Holistic:* a philosophy characterized by comprehension of the parts of something as intimately interconnected and explicable only by reference to the whole.

Beyond swing mechanics, I began to look at the golfer as a human being: a unique person, with a unique body with unique mobility and flexibility, with unique thoughts, feelings, and emotions that all affect their game. There's also one's mentality, one's understanding of strategy, their relationship to pressure and adversity, and their decision making. A human with aspirations and doubts, hopes and fears, innumerable metabolic processes, and a person with an intrinsic fight-or-flight response who has unique reactions to stress. A delicately and perfectly formed person that is capable of anything, yet sometimes hampered by thoughts and maladies. A wonderfully fallible person who strives for better, mostly hopeful, but is often afraid of failure. Most importantly: everyone is a different human being and not just a moving image in my camera.

I changed for the better. I morphed from instructor to coach, and the teacher inside me became determined to share the lesson I learned—an often-overlooked truth—with the world. There's no one-size-fits-all in golf. And focusing just on the swing leaves out many other factors that affect performance.

After many years of trying to get my message out, with sporadic success, I happened on the chance to do a podcast for the PGA Tour.

I started to write a few instructional editorial pieces for PGATour.com, a series which a savvy editor decided to call "On the Mark." Those articles soon grew into an opportunity in a new format: we started a podcast with the same name, and I made it my mission to grow the podcast's reach, with the vision of introducing the listeners around the world to what we can all learn from the best tour pros and teaching pros. We shouldn't simply copy the best, but we should apply what we learn from them to our own swings and games.

It was a lofty goal, forged by my childhood experiences, when golf instruction and insight was in short supply. Back then, I had only seen or heard from leading golfers and instructors in magazines and on the odd VHS cassette: just a few voices, a few sound bytes, not many perspectives. I endeavored to change that for golfers who wanted to learn. I would bring the best directly to the listener and help them process the lessons. Don't learn from just one or two guys, who you have happened to see play, or whose book you've happened to have read: instead, look far and wide for models and insights, and don't be afraid to take a little here from one, and a little from another, and so on.

My goals with the podcast were simple: to introduce golfers—of all skill levels and stations in the game—to bright minds, while bringing them knowledge and insight with an emphasis on converting it into wisdom and understanding. I was fortunate to bring many of my friends and colleagues—as well as golfers I've admired—onto the podcast. I enjoyed talking with some of the leading instructors of our time, including Butch Harmon, David Leadbetter, Bob Rotella, and Bob Winters, to discover the essence of their work and thoughts on a complete approach to the game of golf. Together, these great minds can unlock certain keys for any player of any ability. They're all acquainted with non-elite golfers, and their advice works well beyond the professional tours. I've also interviewed dozens of current tour pros, including Jordan Spieth, Collin Morikawa, and Max Homa, who are all included in this book. Though they have yet to have reached the midpoint in their careers, they are wise beyond their years. I have also really enjoyed talking to some of the legends of the game from the '80s, '90s, and 2000s, including Fred Couples, Nick Price, Nick Faldo, and Justin Leonard. I learned that what was true then about golf is certainly still true now, and that perhaps there are some important things that some have forgotten or missed in this data-driven era, now obsessed with speed and distance. If you follow their insights in this book—and my commentary to help tie key concepts together—you'll gain a true understanding of how to approach the game in a more holistic way.

In my 25+ years as a golf instructor, I learned that a lot of people *know* things about golf, but they don't really *understand* them. Essentially, they are like how I was in Calculus class: I *knew* every equation and theorem by heart, but I had no idea how to *apply* them. Eventually, when a test was put in front of me, I blanked and panicked, with no idea of which equation to use where. I remember my feelings of inadequacy as I fumbled my way through the tests and got a poor grade. I am relentless about helping golfers to not suffer the same fate. Our approach to golf and game improvement should be more simple, more natural. In other words, not Calculus. Knowing a principle is good, but it'll only help you if you *understand* the principles behind it. And then comes the hard work and commitment: only then will it begin to work for you.

Knowledge is important, but you need the perspective, wisdom, and understanding to know what is applicable to you and your game, and whether it will lead to your success. You'll hear me reference that often on my podcast, and in these pages. A true teacher is one who helps others learn how to understand themselves, analyze themselves, and then teach themselves. Like the old saying: Rather than give a man a fish, teach him how to do it himself. And don't just teach him one fishing style, see what works best for him: where he lives, with the fish he wants to catch, and what wrist- and upper-arm strength he has. Let's go further: show him where his best chances are, what is his best approach to take, and what to do when he's failing.

This book is a collection of the many incredible insights we have been fortunate enough to introduce. I wrote it with the intention of helping you improve from the top of your head to the tip of your toes. It's not just thinking about grip or wrist position at impact. Among other things, it's how you move your body, feel your body, use your mind, stick to changes, be your biggest fan, and be grateful along the way. It's also written with a practical mindset: not just theories, but actual guidance to help you improve your understanding of how you improve from tee to green and hole to hole. In short, my approach here is holistic, and I hope it'll ignite something in your understanding, so that you can experience more clarity, improve your game, have more fun, shoot lower scores, and enjoy this wonderful game of golf even more. You can become your own instructor—or as I prefer, coach—to know what works for you.

Golf is a game that has taken me many places and given me countless experiences I could have never imagined when I was a young boy in Somerset West, in South Africa. I've seen a lot of trends and changes in my career, and I have seen what has stuck, what has lasted, what has worked. Over my blessed career, the golf world has opened itself to me, and now I want to open it for you.

I think in teaching there has to be a way you think about things. There's two things you can do: you can teach golf to people, or you can teach people to play golf.

Butch Harmon

1

Butch Harmon

Not Easy, But Simple

For many in the golf world, Butch Harmon is heralded as the preeminent golf instructor of our era. He has not only guided many blue-chip golfers to the top of the game as well as to major championship success, he's also taught or influenced many instructors along the way. There's no such thing as a cookie-cutter approach with Butch: he truly studies each student's game and then customizes his instruction to cater to that player. His approach is congenial and simple, and he blends technical instruction with a playing element that is digestible and easy to apply.

Since I'm after a holistic approach to golf instruction, Butch is a great person to start with. Golf requires many modifications to the swing, stance, posture, and alignment to overcome different challenges and opportunities over the course of 18 holes, so why just focus on one? Every lesson I have seen him give is always guided by the premise that the adjustment or change will be measured by performance under pressure on the golf course.

Butch's appearance on my *On the Mark* podcast was certainly one of the most popular episodes, and countless people have gleaned insight and game-changing tips from what he calls the "pearls" of wisdom he learned from his father, Claude, a man whom Butch called "the greatest instructor that's ever lived." The apple doesn't fall far from the tree.

Butch is an incredible storyteller, and when he's around, he's always the center of the conversation, regaling listeners with funny, yet poignant stories. He's also a great listener: an important skill for all instructors. Butch kicked off our chat on the podcast with a funny story about how his father taught him and his brothers how to control a draw. (Butch's father played a lot of golf with Ben Hogan, and both legends learned to control the dreaded hook.) Similar to Hogan, there's first a lot of focus on wrist position. Butch recalls that his father Claude *"believed very strongly in club path and clubface angle, very similar to the great John Jacobs. And I think what I've learned the most in my golfing career were from my dad and John Jacobs. And he used to talk about the back of the left hand for a right-handed golfer, the bow and the left wrist, keeping the clubface square through impact. His line was, 'You see boys, when I hit it, I've got Bethlehem Steel down here in the left wrist. You boys have linguini in there, coming in there flopping all over the place."* The story is worth a listen, given it was loaded with laughs, but the lesson and the visual are so effective. Imagine cooked linguini: it's all floppy with no structure at all. Now image steel: strong, immoveable, reliable. If your lead wrist is like steel through impact, imagine how strong and reliable its influence would be on the clubface.

The wrists and the hands are the last point in the

chain of communication with the clubhead. And the clubhead is the only medium with which you communicate with the golf ball. In other words, if you want to hit better shots, stop worrying about other swing thoughts like *keep your head down* or *shift your weight*. Instead, focus on your wrists and hands, and their influence on the clubface.

Butch built on that premise, and he talked about wrist conditions and how they affect open and shut'clubfaces. He understood that not all great golfers played with the same grip or wrist positions, and he wanted to learn why. He shared modern examples like Fred Couples, Jon Rahm, and Brooks Koepka: *"As you know, Mark, people think just because your left wrist is bowed [in flexion], that that means the clubface has got to be shut. If you think about it, a lot of it depends on your grip. If you've got a fairly neutral grip, and not too strong, and you have it bowed, the clubface isn't going to be as shut as you think. Now, if you've got a really strong grip like Fred Couples does, he couldn't play from that bowed position. That's why you see his left wrist is more cupped, because his grip so strong. So a lot of times, a player's grip helps you understand where they need to be at the top of the swing."*

I probed Butch on the fact that none of the players he ever taught had swings that resemble a consistent Butch Harmon style or method. I offered this quotation from his father Claude: *"There's only one position in the swing that matters, and that's impact. Everything else is window dressing."* Butch quickly responded, *"I think in teaching there has to be a way you think about things. There's two things you can do: you can teach golf to people, or you can teach people to play golf. Our family believes we're trying to teach people to play golf. We're not trying to teach you a golf swing, we're trying to teach you to play golf. Because everybody's different. I can remember in my 10 years of working with*

Tiger Woods, everybody that came to me said, 'Okay, I want to swing like Tiger Woods,' and I said, 'No kidding! So do I, but unless I can climb in his body, that's not possible.' I said, 'I gotta make you swing the best you can swing.'"

He continued, sharing the family teaching ethos: "*The way we were taught by our father was to never take away what someone does naturally, just make it better. And so that's how we—my brothers and I, anybody who's ever worked for any of us—the way we teach all the young assistants. ... Teach people to play golf, don't teach golf swing.*"

Building on this pearl of Butch's, one of the biggest errors I see golfers—of all skill levels—make is adopting the misguided belief that if one changes one's golf swing, then scores are guaranteed to improve. In my 25+ years of teaching golf, I have seen more than my share of players regress after focusing solely on swing changes and adjustments.

There's more to golf than the golf swing. Consider this: a round of golf is like a test—an examination—and the questions are ever-changing. There are mental and emotional questions, skill questions, decision-making risk and reward questions, and of course execution questions. Like me in Calculus class, they might know the theory or equation, but they don't know how or when to apply it.

Golf is not played in a vacuum, or even an indoor arena. Indeed, the golf course is a constantly moving palette, and no course is the same, and the examination is fickle. Golf is a game played with 14 different implements, on 18 different holes, under varying conditions, both overhead and underfoot. As a result, the golfer—in search of success—should be prepared for any eventuality. As a result, if success—measured by score—is the goal, then you ought to prepare for every question that may be asked.

Sadly, however, the lion's share of golfers mistakenly think that hitting a bucket of balls from a level lie with a 7-iron equates to productive practice. The very same golfers may believe that if they hit a bunch of balls with their driver, their scores will magically lower. Further, most somewhat advanced golfers seem to believe that a swing adjustment or change is the route to success and better scores. As a career golf instructor, I believe that approach is not only misguided but intellectually lazy. Goodness knows, I have seen thousands of functionally sound golf swings that have rarely produced the commensurate scores.

As Butch pointed out, he likes to teach people to play golf. That means being able to hit an iron shot from on either a tight hardpan lie, or from a divot. It means having the ability to flight a shot lower into the wind or elevate a ball when downwind. That means playing off uneven lies, in capricious winds, and of course, under pressure. Playing golf is not just about making pretty golf swings.

When you begin to make swing changes, don't just make adjustments because your swing looks funny or wrong. Butch was unwavering in this observation: *"Go to the World Golf Hall of Fame, because there are hundreds of strange looking swings in there. But they all work, because the secret of golf is repetition."* He added, *"The common thread is getting the club squared at impact and being able to repeat it time and time again."*

I want to stress that if you are making a swing adjustment to straighten out a slice, or to improve a habitual toe-strike, or whatever the malady may be, you should remember to never change something you do naturally. You should just strive to make it a little better and a little more consistent. And only change something if it will make you more capable of repeating the motion under pressure.

For what it's worth, I will forever maintain—and

this is something I learned way back when—that a golf swing is measured with three simple metrics, not launch-monitor metrics. These are the basic questions you should ask of your swing:

- Does the clubface square up at contact?
- Does the swing generate maximum speed for minimum effort?
- Does the swing repeat under pressure?

If you answer 'yes' to these questions, then your swing is functional and capable of producing quality and timely shots.

As this point, I should reiterate Harmon's premise of improving golf swings: do not change something that comes naturally. Put another way, do not suppress the athlete within! I know that may sound overly simplistic. The truth is, it should. Meditate on how the late greats figured out swing adjustments without technology, video, or data. Here's more on that from Butch: *"I've been fortunate enough to work with all the great players … , [and] I learn as much from them as they learned from me, and that just made me better at my job. You know, the old-timers, the people I grew up with, they made the game very simple. They talked about just a position here to do this. Nowadays, they got all this ground force, and hit up on it, and all these angles, and Trackman says you are 'four degrees from the inside and three degrees down.' Now why the hell don't you tell the guy why he's doing that, instead of throwing out some numbers there?"*

A strong teacher is a strong learner, who never stops seeking to learn. And this approach allows instructors to adopt a more holistic and personalized approach.

Never stop asking *how* and *why*. Data has a way of making us feel like the answer is in the numbers, but they often aren't. You don't need to be a data analyst to find what works for you: it's actually simpler than that. I couldn't help but laugh when Butch recounted this 'pearl' from his father *"to show you how simple the old-timers thought and how I think. My dad used to have a scenario: he says, 'Let me explain something to you. This is how simple golf can be. If you have a one-shot lead in a golf tournament, and you're standing on the 18th tee at Pebble Beach. If the heel gets to the ball before the toe, you win. If the toe gets to the ball before the heel, you lose. It's that simple.' And we would say, 'Well Dad, how do you want me to do that?' [He says,] 'I don't care how you do it. Just do it!' You see that's the way the old-timers thought. They didn't have all this technology and all this other stuff, and all these things go into their heads."* So brilliant. So funny. So poignant. So true!

Butch believes that golf should be taught at a second-grade level, because it can feel like such a difficult game. He also believes that golf instructors should pick out the one thing—or as he calls it "the cancer in the swing"—that's causing the largest problem. Teachers should find that one thing that will have a knock-on effect on three or four other things in the swing.

Butch also stresses that all students, no matter who they are, should have healthy expectations of results, because *"change takes time. And I try and tell the average players, that we teach, that bad shots are part of the process. Understanding the bad shots is part of the process of how you're going to get better."*

Butch referenced his work with Tiger Woods after Woods' 1997 Masters victory, that it took a while for Tiger to get used to the new position at the top of the swing. In fact, during the 1998 season, Woods won only one time. Butch explains, *"The average person doesn't realize that it takes time to change. It takes time for the change to feel comfortable. [With] the best player in the world, it takes him almost the whole season to feel comfortable with a change, how the heck could a 15-handicap think he's gonna take one lesson and all of a sudden, he's gonna win the club championship? I mean, that's not what's gonna happen."* Patience and perspective are key. If you don't have both, you'll just become frustrated and confused and quit before the real results come.

One more thing as it pertains to swing work and changes: you should never confuse technique with skill. Golf is a game of spin and—by extension—a game of skill. I really don't care how well you "shallow" the club on the downswing, if you don't have the skill to land the club in the correct area with the face pointing in the appropriate direction relative to the swing path to facilitate a certain trajectory. The truth is that you could shallow the club like Ben Hogan, but if you don't get the clubface aligned with the swing path, you will never hit the shots you're looking for.

Learn to hit hooks and fades. Spend time creating shots on the practice area. Often straightening your golf shots is as simple as creating the opposite spin to your problem. Butch Harmon agreed with me on this: *"I believe in opposites. If you're hitting slices, I'm going to try and make you hit a hook. And you hit hooks, I'm gonna try and make you hit a slice, and you'll meet in the middle. You have to understand what they're doing that causes the path to be out-to-in too much, in-to-out or whatever it is. But if you go the opposites, it's amazing how they meet in the middle, and it makes things easier."*

As Butch stressed, learn to play golf, not the golf swing. You should learn from the best, but also learn how to apply what you learn. See what will work for you and what doesn't. Measure what works from the results they produce. And never stop learning. It's not easy, but it's simple.

I think you gotta figure out your own game and then really catch onto a teacher that figures your game out. Not what he wants you to do.

Fred Couples

2

Fred Couples

EASY DOES IT: BE YOURSELF

Fred Couples is one of the greatest, most naturally gifted golfers of all time. The hall-of-famer and 1992 Masters champion is also an all-time human being and a joy to be around, so when Bridgestone Golf invited me to spend time with him and record an episode of the *On the Mark* podcast, I jumped at the opportunity.

Spending time with Freddie is easy. His light-hearted, relaxed manner makes him a tremendous storyteller, and he weaves yarns that have you hooked from the start through the finish, even though often the finish has nothing to do with the beginning. It's probably why Fred is the center of the conversation on most PGA Tour or Champions Tour ranges or putting greens. That said, he brings an incisive, yet simple wisdom to the game and how he plays it. He is curious and not afraid to learn new things, and I was somewhat surprised how interested he was in my opinion on golf instruction during our time together.

Freddie had me enthralled for about an hour as he regaled me with stories and anecdotes from his life in golf, his Masters win, how he learns, and how plays the game.

It's always a good idea to start at the beginning, and I asked Fred to reminisce about his days as a junior golfer in Seattle, Washington. He spoke fondly of his childhood days and how he was into baseball and soccer. Golf was not his first interest though, and he just learned to play the game before he enhanced his technique: *"I'll tell you what [I learned] as I got to be a better young nine- and ten-year-old player. I grew up on a par-three course: Jefferson Park. There's one short par four, but all great par threes with pop-up greens. And then it had an 18-hole course. So going backwards just for a second ... you get different lies. You get bunkers that aren't raked, because it's a public facility. And you're taught a lot of things ... It just was a blast for me to play. I had so many friends that played. So growing up on a public course, you know, I played with everybody. I think if I grew up [at] a country club, I probably would play with most young juniors. But I learned to grow up, you know, any little mistakes as a 13-year-old, these 30- and 40-year-olds wouldn't want to be around some punk."*

The best way to learn the game—for juniors and adults alike—is to play alongside better golfers. I remember as I got into golf at 14, my brother Trevor— who is 9 years my junior—would tag along with me and my friends. He was 5! Suffice it to say, Trevor quickly learned how to play fast and grind for scores. Necessity being the mother of invention, he also quickly learned that the only way he could compete with the big kids was to develop a dynamite short game. Trevor would spend hours on the putting green, honing his skill and taking money off adults in putting contests. Then when Trevor grew bigger and stronger, all bets were off. His newfound power off the tee—coupled with his electric skills on and around the greens—turned into a winning combination. The rest was history.

Learning to play golf takes many facets, including developing the skill of being able to play from any lie.

Couples mentioned learning in unraked bunkers. For many, that would be an irritation, but for others it's an opportunity to learn and develop a complete skill set. As the great Bobby Jones once said, "You get bad breaks from good shots; you get good breaks from bad shots, but you have to play the ball as it lies."

Too many golfers make the mistake of playing the ball up. Now there are exceptions of course, but when you are out on the course, the only way you can grow as a player is by playing from different lies, unusual lies, bad lies, also a plugged lie in a bunker, a barren lie or divot in the fairway, and a ball behind a tree or bush. You need to learn how to overcome all of these, and the only way to learn how is by putting yourself in that uncomfortable situation. If I've said it once, I have said it a thousand times: Growth only happens outside of your comfort zone.

So don't be afraid of playing out of the bad lie. Doing so will only make you a more complete and confident player in the long run. For what it's worth, Freddie mentioned that as teenagers, he and his friends would play their 18-hole course from the tips every time. In his words, they teed off one yard away from the back of every tee, and they played the ball down in all weather conditions. You can't improve if you take shortcuts and make things easier for yourself.

Now to that that silky, languid Fred Couples swing that stamped out power-fades with monotonous regularity. Couples' swing, with its enviable rhythmic flow, its flash of speed through impact, and that cool, almost laissez-faire finish—that just about everyone has tried to emulate—has not always hit a left-to-right pattern. Couples credited his development by citing his athletic instincts from playing soccer and baseball, as well as emulating an older golfer and friend. Fred said, *"When I first started playing, I was this little kid with a lot of clubhead speed [from baseball], and I used to hit these*

kind of low draws to get it to go far. That's how I fig-
ured ... it was the only way I could [keep up], you know.
And so then with help, as I got to be 12 and 13, I just
generated a little better swing through the ball, and I
started hitting it higher. Because most of the time in Seat-
tle, you know, the ball would plug."

Couples said he learned to mimic a friend's swing. He
explained, *"I've always hit the ball a certain trajectory,*
but you are right, when I first started, I manufactured
a swing ... by watching this guy, [my friend] Steve, who
hit it a long way." Stealing with your eyes—picking up
ideas from the better players you play with—is never
a bad thing. As a matter of fact, I often recommend it
to golfers of all levels: Find a great golfer near you and
take something they do that can work for you. You'll
hear all of the tour pros in this book talk about the importance of learning from others.

Imitation is the sincerest form of flattery, but it's
also a great way to learn. Think of any young child. A lot
of a child's movement and motor skills are learned not
by being *told* how, but purely by watching and copying others. In terms of golfers, Phil Mickelson springs
to mind. As a young child, Mickelson, who is a natural
right-hander, copied his right-handed father's swing
like a mirror image. As we have all seen, that was highly
beneficial to Phil, and it can to anybody who is trying to
improve. Even advanced golfers watch, emulate, feel,
and replicate. Heck, I remember as a young golfer making countless swings while looking at my reflection in
the living room window. I recall Nick Faldo saying to
me that he wishes he had spent more time practicing in
front of a mirror.

As Couples continued to share his thoughts on development, he admitted that he would watch other
professional golfers such as Ernie Els, Nick Faldo, Tom
Purtzer, and Larry Mize, and how they approached
their swing, how they hit balls. Again, copying some-

one's swing isn't what works, it's replicating elements of someone's swing that work for you and your body. For Fred, it was how a Purtzer cleared through the ball, if Couples wanted to work on clearing his hips through impact. If he wanted to work on rhythm and momentum, he'd watch Larry Mize's swing. It's not trying to duplicate any one swing: it's picking certain things that certain players do well.

In a genius sort of way, Fred could focus on particular aspects of different swings, ones that were not only great models, but could also work for his body and swing. I'd recommend this approach to all golfers as well. For example, if you are trying to rotate more in your backswing, find a model that does it very well, and focus on only that, and allow it to settle into your psyche.

Back to Freddie. It's hard to believe, given his carefree manner, that he could ever be dogmatic. But in a way, he was forthright when it came to his feelings on golf instruction and teaching: *"I think you got to figure out your own game and then really catch on to a teacher that figures your game out, not what he wants you to do. But I think one of the things that a good teacher does is he works with his students. And again, sometimes I don't catch on to things. And I look right at Paul [Marchand— Couples' long-time coach] whether I was 30 years old or 50, and I say, 'I'm not catching on, let's just go another direction here.'"*

This is classic Couples, and I believe there's a valuable lesson here: if you are taking a lesson, you have to find somebody who will work with you and what you can do physically. Further, as Fred mentioned, if you don't think you can do it after focused and conscious effort, it may be time to find another way around the problem. I can't help but think that if Freddie was not inclined that way, it's likely he would not have turned into the tremendous golfer he became.

Let's be honest, Couples' swing is idiosyncratic. From his late hip turn going back, to his lifted, upright arm movement in the backswing, to his cupped wrist at the top, to his super-fast re-hinge of the wrists in the follow-through: these are all things that a teacher with limited experience would want to change. They aren't textbook at all, but Freddie can repeat them with near-exact accuracy. But it fits him.

Couples also shared that when he'd go for a lesson with his long-time teacher, Paul Marchand, he would make a multi-day outing of it, because change did not come easy to him. Fred explains, *"I'd go to see Paul, or work with Paul for two or three days. I used to love that. Not a one-hour or two-hour lesson, it would be two-and-a-half full days. Because it took me a while."* Couple that extra coaching time spent with Fred's proclivity to abandon a change and find an alternate option, and you have a recipe for a successful golf lesson.

If an uber-talented golfer like Fred Couples believes that he can't learn—and change—something in a one-or two-hour lesson, then it's likely that you won't be able to either. Be patient with finding what works for you. I've taught many elite golfers, and my whole-hearted conviction is: Every change takes time to settle and become a habit. Golfers need to approach swing changes with this belief, because if they aren't, there's a very real chance that the learner will abandon the change before it has ripened. And when that occurs, the result is a golfer who is continually on the coaching carousel, always looking for the next answer or secret. Continuity never has a chance to be established, and at the end of the carousel ride, you have a lesson-taker who gets off frustrated and unaware of who they really are as a player. Worse yet, that well-meaning lesson-taker begins to hate the game.

Avoid the carousel. Remember, a green peach is still a peach. Even though it may not taste as good as a ripened peach, it's still good. And if you give it a little time to ripen, then you will be able to enjoy its taste and nourishment. Now that's not to say that you shouldn't see quick improvements in the way the ball is struck, or how it flies, if you're making the appropriate change. Things should begin to improve the instant the change is recommended and then applied (correctly). The "greenness" you may experience is how it works on the course, or how you're able to trust it and stick to it under pressure.

Remember too that a peach does not ripen in the blink of an eye. Its ripening is a steady process that occurs under the right conditions. Think of a swing change this way. If you improve by 1% every day, you'll be 100% better in about three months. All the greats that I've talked to—including Nick Faldo—have stressed that very point.

Back to swing technique. Fred Couples has never been—and is still not hand-cuffed—by technical thoughts: *"to be honest with you, most everything [with me] was alignment, set-up ... and for me that would be wide open, and where the ball position is. And sometimes by getting it open, I would have it [ball-position] so far forward that I'd get screwed up."* Freddie is all about feel and his sense for timing, speed, and tempo is otherworldly. Consider this observation: *"there's certain ways I'm more feel. So I want to actually feel the ball fly off the face of my club. If I'm gonna hit a 7-iron, you know, make-up numbers, 165 [yards], I am going to really clear hard through the ball. And I wouldn't want the face and the ball touching that long. If I'm going to hit it 157 [yards], I feel like the ball is staying on the face longer."* Please re-read that statement and meditate on it for a little while. Can you sense how long the ball is on the clubface? If not, maybe you should try to become a little more aware from a sensory standpoint. It will probably help you with distance control—if not with the long clubs, at least do it with the putter.

Even though Couples is an all-time feel player, there are even some feels that he doesn't feel. Fred shared, *"so it's just one of those things when you hear Jack Nicklaus say, 'well, you know, to hit it lower, I hit it one groove lower.' I can't appreciate that, because it's not something I thought about, but I can tell you that if I'm maneuvering the ball around the course, because my swing, when I'm hitting a punch shot, I never had a sawed-off finish. It was always long, and my finish was long ... and I am varying the speed through the ball. And with most long clubs, I could stand wide open and hit a driver."* Unlike many golfers in his generation, Fred didn't try to do everything as Jack did it. Instead, Fred does Fred. And you should do you. Always.

So if you are seeking to improve *your* game, make this the capstone and guiding light to every lesson, or golf-tip you ever take: You have to be true to what you are able to consistently do. There's a common saying where I'm from: "a leopard never changes its spots," meaning you're unlikely to make wholesale changes to your swing unless you are fantastically diligent, have oodles of time, and are dedicated to it for the long haul. (For what it's worth, Couples has also worked with Butch Harmon, but all great golfers—including Freddie— never try to change their spots. They learn what they can learn from different players and instructors.)

Remember that real change takes time. Just one 60-minute lesson won't do. Even Tiger Woods took a while for his first swing overhaul—under the guidance of Butch Harmon—to stick. If you do something half a million times, like Tiger has in swinging a club a certain way, you can imagine that it'll take some time for muscles and hands and hips to adjust. What's more, Woods was working every day, all day, practicing, training, and having periodic check-ups ... and he's more than a little more talented and physically gifted than we are.

As a golf teacher and lover of the game, it's my hope that everybody plays well, and lessons are the best way to improve. The truth, however, is that given time and commitment restraints, the average amateur golfer is probably not going to be able to make drastic changes to their swing. We have time limitations, physical limitations, and—let's face it—mental limitations. We have to work with what we have, and if you do that, I think you'll find that you gain more realistic benefits than pretending you're superhuman.

What is more advisable—and definitely has a better chance of success—is for golfers to pay heed to Freddie's counsel. You aren't built or as athletically inclined as Jon Rahm, or Rory McIlroy, or Nelly Korda, nor do you have access to their time and resources. You don't—and can't—spend as much time with workouts, stretching, diet, psychology, and practice as they do. So don't try and swing like them. Rather, connect with a teacher or a professional who can work with what you can consistently do.

Remember the Jim Furyk anecdote in my introduction? To this day, Furyk's odd-looking—but seriously efficient—swing is producing reliable shots under pressure. Indeed if I were to add a fourth measure to my questions, the effectiveness of any golf swing should be assessed by answering this question: "will this swing stand the test of time?"

The thing about the test of time, though, is that it is principally governed by how an individual ages. That's why it is crucial, in my opinion, to be acutely aware of what a learner is capable of doing, physically, without too much physical strain or exertion. What good is a swing change if it creates back problems, or something else?

As a lesson-taker—or even the golfer who is searching for some sort of swing-saving tip from a friend—it's important to respect Fred's recommendation: *"to figure your own game out"* and then find a teacher who works within your abilities.

If you watch Freddie's golf swing through the years, you'll see a definite thread, a consistency to its approach. The only things that have changed are the length and the speed—and both of those are functions of Father Time being unbeaten.

There's a newish saying that goes, "Be yourself: everyone else is already taken." In fact, many of Fred's hall-of-fame counterparts are and were inclined the same way. Be like Fred, which means: be yourself. Swing your swing!

I don't know how, but the golf ball knows what you're thinking. … Most tour players will say that the ball usually goes where their last thought is, so if I can get my head in the right place, I will be in pretty good shape.

Dr. Bob Rotella

3

Bob Rotella

PLAYING GOLF INSTEAD OF GOLF SWING

Just like Butch Harmon, Dr. Bob Rotella is arguably the leading figure in his area of golf instruction. Known as the godfather of sports psychology in golf, Dr. Bob has been sought out by countless legends, including Pat Bradley, Tom Kite, Nick Price, and Davis Love III. He has also guided major champions such as Padraig Harrington, Jim Furyk, and Rory McIlroy to success. His expertise, experience, and knowledge set him apart. He has authored many books on the mental game, and I have had the luxury of many on-course chats with Dr. Bob. It was a thrill to have him share his insights on my podcast.

Every insight about the mental side of golf that Rotella shared deserves study, but for the sake of this chapter, I have to narrow them down to the essential.

Before I elaborate on his approach to pre-shot thoughts and shot results, I have to acknowledge a statement Dr. Bob made, a truism that is likely to grab your attention and challenge you to improve your skills with your 15th club. Our chat kicked off with me asking him to give an overview of his thoughts on the mental game. He responded, *"the bottom line is, as athletes, we have a free will. We get to choose how we want to think about ourselves, et cetera. We get to choose how we perceive ourselves. We get to choose how we perceive our golf swings, our talent, our games, and you just seem to do a lot better if you're in a great state of mind, rather than an average or mediocre state of mind."*

Dr. Bob elaborated a little further on the importance of having a positive mind and outlook: *"I can tell you this, you don't have a chance if you're negative. And positive thinking doesn't guarantee that you're going to be successful, but it guarantees you that you're going to find out if you have the ability to play at the level you want to play. And, you know, when you're negative, you don't ever get to find out."*

When Rotella shares his wisdom, it immediately prompts our introspection. His observation can be so simple—and we may think, yes of course that is true—but ask yourself, how often are you negative on the range or golf course, regardless of what you know?

Every day—at every moment—we are posed a question about our attitude. Will we look at something in a positive or a negative light. On the golf course, this is especially true. Every shot gives a golfer the choice of responding positively or negatively, and we are certainly capable of being negative about excellent shots. As Rotella says that if you tend to the negative, *"you don't know if it's your game or your talent or your attitude"* that's keeping you from your best performance. They're all interconnected, beginning with your attitude.

Rotella had my mind spinning, and I recounted a

principle he had taught me: What people become depends largely on what they think of themselves. I also mentioned that he had taught me that golfers need to work on their mental games. Dr. Bob responded, *"I think it's very intriguing that people think that they have to work on their physical swing, but they don't think they should have to work on their mental or emotional game."*

Rotella then pivoted to the value of good habits: *"We are very much a victim of habit as human beings. And the bottom line is, I gotta get people to create good habits, and to create good habits you got to do it on a consistent basis, day after day. And eventually it starts becoming pretty habitual to have an optimistic outlook, and think positively, and be decisive and committed over your shots. But it's very easy to get away from it. And so you got to constantly catch it. And I think the more you can catch it when you're a half an inch away, you can really start to separate yourself from people."*

I love how he views an optimistic outlook and positive and decisive commitment to golf shots as a separator. It truly is.

Then consider for a moment how many shots, in your most recent round of golf, that you hit with minimal planning, zero commitment, and a poor attitude. Or how many shots you hit while still having your mind mulling over the three-putt you just had, or a bad tee shot on this hole last time you played it. Every single one of those shots was basically wasted, and if they turned out successful, it was accidentally so, even lucky, in spite of everything you forced yourself to overcome.

The tendency then is to blame the golf swing for the failure. In my opinion, this is an intellectually lazy approach, and it has led to many a golfer trying to "fix" a swing that is not really broken. The mind tells the body what to do, and if you're thinking of a past bad shot, guess what the body will do?

Given my golf instructor's nature to gravitate toward

technique, I always felt that it was hard to work on the mental game. Dr. Bob corrected that thinking: *"It's actually easier to work on it because you could sit in a chair or lie in bed or on a couch or be going for a walk and work on it."*

He elaborated on its difficulty as he continued: *"but it's probably harder for most people, because it's a lot easier to lie to yourself about what's going on inside your head. We can't take a picture of it. It doesn't show up on television. You're the only one who really knows what you're thinking, and so you have to be very honest with yourself."*

Honest self-assessment is imperative to success. PGA Tour players, to a man, use ShotLink data to appropriately assess their performance and then make decisions governing whatever work is necessary for improvement. The problem as it relates the mental game is that there is no real measurement device for the mindset. What is required is brutal and uncomfortable honesty. Dr. Bob shares this insight: *"if someone asked me the #1 thing I see in players that are really successful, it's how unbelievably honest they are about how they know the difference between missing a shot, and missing a shot because they didn't give it a chance because they had some doubt or fear in their head. Or they got distracted, or they let their eyes wander over to the trouble. Or they started thinking about missing a putt, or skulling a chip-shot, or something. And they're very honest about it. I think a lot of people would like to not be honest, because most things in life you can kind of fudge and get away with not being honest."*

Some people think that they should always be positive, and they will blame anything for a bad shot but themselves: it was a gust of wind, the caddie gave a bad yardage, there was a little dirt on the ball, that lie was so unfair, and so on; there's no end to what we can come up with. But what some people don't recognize is that this kind of deflecting of blame is negative thinking as well: believing you only get bad breaks, or that the world is conspiring against you, doesn't do yourself any good either. Instead, taking ownership over your results and being brutally honest with yourself puts you on a path of self-awareness, self-actualization, and self-improvement.

Rotella reminds us that when we work with inanimate objects: a club, a ball, a fairway, and a green that aren't going anywhere, that we should only look at ourselves. These things don't create the outcome: you do. He says, *"I don't know how, but the golf ball knows what you're thinking. It's a funny way of saying that, but it's a really good way to look at the game. When you come to grips with the fact that most of the time the ball is going to go where you're thinking, and if it doesn't go where you're thinking, it is because your thinking has gotten so bad that now you're going to hit the opposite direction. Because you intentionally made sure it didn't go wrong is what I mean."*

What a simple way of looking at the game: the ball is going to go where I'm thinking. It sounds a little hocus-pocus, but you know it's true. You have been there, I am sure. You are over a shot, and you see the bunker short of the green. You talk about how you're going to avoid the bunker, but your brain only hears *bunker.* Then what do you know, a minute later you're grabbing a rake.

The tour pro operates like that too, but the difference is they modify their focus to more constructive and beneficial targets. As Rotella explains, *"Most tour players will say that the ball usually goes where their last thought is, so if I can get my head in the right place I will be in pretty good shape."*

Out on the PGA Tour, pros and caddies, through the ages, have recognized empirically that the ball is likely to travel toward where their last thought—or words—

were. This is best illustrated when you hear player-caddie conversations on television broadcasts. One thing you will *never* hear a caddie say is: "Don't go left ... there is water over there," or "Watch out for the bunker short of the green."

Instead, you'll always hear them speak of a target that's definite and perhaps on the opposite side of the trouble. Something like, "You have a lot of room on the right," or "There's a slope behind the flag that will slow the ball down."

Then, the key is for the player to commit completely to that target, whatever it is. More often than not, if the target is not the flag, you will hear a caddie recommend aiming at a TV tower, or perhaps a tree, or a fan with a bright shirt as the "new" target instead of the flag. Often these new targets are behind the middle of the green, or on the safe side of the target, to account for the odd mishit.

Interestingly, Dr. Bob believes that the origin of most double-crossed shots is when a golfer is caught between the thought of the flag while they are trying to aim away from it. Rotella's work with golfers includes them building the discipline of picking another definitive target when aiming away from the flag.

So, when you are out on the course, indeed even before you go out on the course, clean up your thought-life and most certainly your self-talk. The discipline of learning this skill—which takes practice to master and make a habit—will not necessarily improve a faulty golf swing, but it will most certainly eliminate disasters from your round. When you learn how to do that, you will be surprised at how good your bad day can be.

Speaking of bad days ... golf is beset with those, for players of all levels, and Rotella addressed how to deal with them mentally. He asks, *"How does it make sense that if your stroke or your swing is off that you should also think poorly? That makes no sense! The one thing you can do is commit, and trust your routine and your process."*

Dr. Rotella is normally softly spoken and paternal in his manner, but this statement was dispatched with a little extra spice. He continued, *"It's amazing how many people justify being indecisive or playing with doubt, because their swing's not where they want it. They'll say, 'Well, when I get it in the slot, then I'll think good,' and I'll think, 'Oh, well, anybody could do that.' And, as you know on tour, probably at least 40% of the time, their game isn't where they want it, but you got to be able to score regardless. And I think that's where, you know ... we talked about skills; we talked about competence; at some point you have to have belief that you can get the ball in the hole. It really doesn't have much to do with your skills once you're on the golf course. Yeah, we've done a lot of time preparing them. But once you get on the course, it's like you got to take what you got to go play with."*

It's the gospel truth from Dr. Bob, but sadly a truism overlooked by too many golfers. I saw it play out, week-in and week-out during my 20 years as a college golf coach. All too often, I would see young competitive golfers have a bad stretch of golf (physically), and in their frustration they would throw out the proverbial baby with the bathwater and lose their minds.

Two bad holes would throw them into a tailspin, and things would go from bad to worse. In the end, what should have been a round of 74 or 75 turned into 79 or sometimes worse, effectively plummeting them out of contention, and most certainly ruining a respectable finish.

Nick Price, a Rotella disciple, once told me that he began to win big tournaments and majors when he learned to make his bad day decent. He observed that when he learned to navigate his way around bad physical days—with a constructive, sometimes conservative, but definitely committed mindset and decisions—he kept himself relevant and in the tournament. (We'll learn much more about this from Nick in Chapter 6.)

Getting the most out of any round of golf requires purpose-driven pre-shot routines, a focused mindset, appropriate situational decision-making and positive, uplifting self-talk. It also requires imagination and subconscious reaction and athleticism. Rotella discusses the importance of letting a certain amount of conscious thoughts go: *"It's really a matter of making sure you understand that when you get in competition on a golf course you got to be able to hit golf shots. And so, you got to keep your imagination alive. And most people have a lot of imagination when they're little kids. And over time, they kind of learn how to do everything with their conscious brain. And to be a good golfer you have to learn to do it with your imagination and your subconscious brain, but it takes a lot of trust to do that. But I mean, it's no different than a pianist, when they begin maybe learning how to read notes and where do their fingers go on the piano, and at some point to make beautiful music you have to let go of any of that conscious instruction. You just hear the song in your head, and your hands just go like crazy on the piano and hit all the right keys."*

To that subconscious reaction and allowing the athlete within to thrive, I explored visualization and pre-shot routines with Dr. Bob. He says to find something natural that isn't over complicated: *"We tend to make even visualizing into this really hard, serious, conscious thing that you have to do. And it's really a very unconscious activity. It's just pick a target, [and] it happens. And that's where you'd like to get to. You know, I want to make it as simple as possible. I want people to do whatever comes most natural."*

The human brain is so complex, it can often get in the way on the golf course. He spoke of the power of the brain: *"You don't have to tell your brain that's where*

I want the ball to go. You don't have to actually see it in your mind. Your brain is so brilliant that you pick a target and you're playing golf, your brain unconsciously knows that you're playing golf and wants the ball to go there."

He quickly reiterated after his remark that it is therefore imperative, that if aiming away from a flag or the hole, you need to consciously identify a new target and commit to it—remember his "double-cross" observation.

Regarding the pre-shot routine, Dr. Bob was pretty clear: it must be short and simple, and it must be for every part of the game: *"I'd make it as short and simple as possible. I don't care if you stand behind the ball or stand next to it. But don't step up to the ball until you pick the target and committed to the shot you're going to hit. And then I would say if I had my choice, I mean, I would say take one look and one waggle or two looks and two waggles. I mean, that'd be a very simple routine for most people. The longer you take, the more discipline you have to have to not get distracted, and you certainly give yourself more opportunity to be distracted and get your muscles in your body tight. ... You want to have a routine with every part of your game. I don't care if it's a little different for your long game versus putting versus pitching, but you need to have a routine. ... I'd like them to have whether it's a waggle, or a knee kick, or head turn, but you need something as a trigger. That's really simple for you to do that keeps you moving and keeps you from getting too stationary."*

If this all seems too simple to believe, you should go and download my *On the Mark* episode with Bob Rotella. Listening to him for 30 minutes or so is good for the soul. He is a wise man who truly understands golf and competition, and most importantly, how it combines with the human psyche and the human nature.

Don't ever expect to make no mistakes. Every player

makes them in every round, and it's how you handle them that keeps a good round going. Rotella describes a potential mental process: *"First of all, before anyone goes the 1st tee, I want them to already have admitted that golf is a game of mistakes, and so they're going to make plenty of mistakes. I think the second thing is you got to be prepared: how am I going to respond to my mistakes? Are you going to beat yourself up and decide you're stupid, or a jerk, or a choke? Or are you going to just accept [the mistakes]. So I'm very much into wanting people to prepare their mind that they're going to make mistakes, but you're not going to be bothered by it. You have to get to the point where they just don't mean anything to you."*

As Bob Rotella always says, *"train and trust."*

I have experienced stuff like that where it's like, look stuff happened. What are you going to do? You still have golf left, so you may as well be trying to hit every shot where you're looking, and every putt where you're looking. Just like [I] tried to before when it didn't work out, but doesn't mean it won't now.

Jordan Spieth

4

Jordan Spieth

GETTING UNCOMFORTABLE TO BE COMFORTABLE

Jordan Spieth is one of the most talented and exciting players of his generation. The American superstar roared onto the PGA Tour, making an immediate impact. He became a household name in the blink of an eye.

Spieth won his first PGA Tour event—the 2013 John Deere Classic—as a 19-year-old, showing the poise and professionalism of a veteran. He built on that win and grew in stature, notching his first major victory as a 21-year-old in the 2015 Masters Tournament.

Jordan's momentum kept rolling. A few months later, Spieth outlasted Dustin Johnson, Branden Grace, Louis Oosthuizen, and Adam Scott to win the U.S. Open at Chambers Bay. His triumph made him the youngest U.S. Open champion since Bobby Jones in 1923.

Jordan added multiple tour victories and another major at the 2017 Open Championship at Royal Birkdale, cementing him as one of the best Americans ever. And he's not done yet. Spieth has re-invented himself and is clawing his way back to the top of the world's game after battling through a slump in form. After chatting with him recently, and seeing his form over the past year, it's clear he's positioned well—physically and mentally—to win more tournaments soon.

All the while, Jordan is polite, eloquent, candid, and wise beyond his years. He's a tremendous interviewee, and I was thrilled to talk with him on my podcast.

As a player, he's exciting, dynamic, and capable of anything. Fans have likened his style of play to that of a rollercoaster ride. His skill on and around the greens is magical, and I marvel when I watch him with a wedge or putter in his hand. Indeed, he chips in more than any other golfer I have ever watched.

I recall one particular CBS broadcast when I was covering his group. He had missed a green in regulation and had found himself in a pretty awkward spot. I remember my interaction with Jim Nantz vividly. Jim set up the shot and asked me about the situation in which Jordan found himself in. I responded with something to the effect of, "Jim, I actually look forward to Jordan missing greens so I can see what he does next." Nantz responded, "Me too, Mark." Jordan wielded his trusty lob wedge like it was Excalibur. He spun a pitch shot that shaved the edge of the hole before coming to rest a few feet from the hole. It nearly went in. Both Jim Nantz and I giggled at the spectacle. I think history will describe Jordan in the same fashion as the great Seve Ballesteros: a passionate player who's stunning watch, and a magician with a wedge.

Jordan explains that his talent comes from his mother and father: *"Both of my parents played Division I college sports. My mom played basketball and my dad played baseball. I have a brother that's 18 months younger than me, and we just grew up with a ball in our hands. So we were playing basketball, baseball, soccer, football. Golf ended up being something that I took up around when my brother was born. It [was] just kind of an activity to keep myself busy.*" I know of so many successful golfers who grew up spending hours during each non-school day at the course. It's a wonderful sport to learn for so many reasons, including the fact that the golf course is a wonderful babysitter, too. It was how my brother and I grew up, and I wouldn't trade it for the world.

Jordan's first love was baseball. He was naturally left-handed and played baseball and basketball until he was about 13 when his love of golf blossomed. He recalls, *"I just remember what was so cool about it was I felt like [when] I went to the course. I felt like I was getting better. I was having fun doing so. We were playing. I was dropped off at 8:30 in the morning. I would hit some balls, we'd go play 18, and we'd go play some basketball. We'd play some football in the parking lot. Go back, eat lunch, hit some more balls, and go play again. I was like, man, I just I'm having a lot of fun these days.*" Parents: this is a wonderful way for any aspirant athlete to grow up.

Over the summer, I watch the kids at my home club in Georgia. They show up in the morning, go and play a few holes, then they go to the pool and swim and eat lunch at the hottest part of the day. Then they go and practice and play again. Then they might play pickleball at dusk. They are just kids—young athletes—having fun. All the while they're becoming healthy, fit, well-adjusted athletes who play golf. The well-rounded, well-adjusted child can deal with the rigors of competitive golf the best. Allow your child this independent growing-up time. If they really have what it takes, it will come out. Don't try to force it. If you do, you run the risk of driving your child away from our great game, a game that will expose them to lessons for a lifetime and an incredible network of people as well.

I'm a firm believer in the value of competition.

Whether an adult or a young person, there's no better way to accelerate development than to play with better golfers. Remember Fred Couples said about his childhood days, playing with older and better golfers? I quizzed Jordan on competition and being a competitor, because from my point of view, there are few like Jordan. When the pressure gets up and he gets a sniff of the lead, he seems to click into another gear. At times he almost wills the ball into the hole. He responded, *"I started to really enjoy having the ball in my hands. You know, I think I've spoken to that before. It's like when I played other sports, somebody was better on the team, and they always got the last shot. And in golf it was all on you, and that's what I love."* Though some believe that the nature of wanting the ball in your hands is somewhat innate, it can be learned and trained. The major learning factor is not necessarily only having the skill to pull off the shot: it's also wanting to take on the pressure and being prepared if you fail. You have to be prepared to face the outcome, the consequence of the ball not going in the hole, or in the hoop, or between the posts. It comes from allowing the mindset to pivot to a place of freedom, specifically the freedom to fail. Developing the mindset that is okay with being less than okay after a failure is what gives a star like Jordan Spieth the ability to take the ball and attempt to do something special when the chips are down. You have nothing to fear except fear itself.

If you are struggling to be that person, then you'd be well served to take Ben Hogan's advice to heart. Hogan argued that the most important shot was the "next one." If you let this insight to settle in your psyche, you'll free yourself up to attempt that pivotal shot, swinging freely, and giving the shot the best possible chance of success. Start small with this mindset shift. Do this on the greens. Over every putt inside 10 feet, allow your stroke to free up to a point where you give the ball enough speed to miss—if possible, on the high side. No more limping makeable putts up short of the hole: give those babies a chance. Indeed, Jordan mentioned that he tries to hole every shot on and around the greens.

A great competitor must love the pressure of competition, as Spieth does. Jordan shared, *"Yeah, I think that's what excites me. At the same time, sometimes maybe too much excitement, and I just can get away from standard stuff. I've had plenty of scenarios where I've made it look easy, and I've had some where I made it look really hard. But that's golf. But yeah, I think it's just nice to start getting somewhat giddy when I get towards the top, because your confidence is there and all of a sudden you're competing."* I love that you can see the excitement in Jordan's demeanor when he's in contention. He gets more chatty, more animated, and more invested. He's certainly never trying to temper this natural reaction to the environment. He's true to who he is, and he just lets it all hang out. This is so admirable, and I would challenge you to be yourself as often as possible too. Arnold Palmer talked about "swinging your swing, not some idea of a swing." I like that, but I challenge you—as the saying goes—to "be yourself, not some idea of who you are supposed to be." The alternative has short legs and a less-than-favorable outcome.

While Spieth's competitive and athletic instincts are tremendous, his short-game skill sets him apart. I was wanting to get the secrets from the wizard's mouth, and I didn't take long to guide our conversation to how Jordan hits chips, pitches, and bunker shots. I kicked it off by having him revisit his bunker shot heroics on the 72nd hole of the 2013 John Deere Classic. Jordan remembered, *"I found myself in that bunker, and honestly there was just no point in trying to make par, because I knew that if I make par, I have no chance of winning. Winning is all that mattered to me at that point, considering I had already played well, [and] the only way to actually get full status [on the PGA Tour] away from my temporary membership was to win."* Jordan had already done enough in his first few starts on the PGA Tour, but as a competitor, he wanted more. The only way he could qualify for the FedEx Cup Playoffs that year was by winning, as that would earn him full tour membership status. He called it playing with "freedom and aggression."

Jordan reminded me of a common adage: never up, never in. If you don't give the ball a chance of getting to the hole, you'll never make it in the hole. He said of his mentality before that epic bunker shot, *"The point was it was going to get to the hole, because there was no reason for it not to. I luckily approach most of my shots I hit around the greens that way; you know it doesn't have a chance to get stopped, or go in if it doesn't get there."*

Jordan's insight reminds me of what I call the #1 Rule in Golf: a ball will roll down a hill. Too many golfers miss putts, or chips and pitches because they never allow enough for the slope and tilt of the ground. They worry about going past the hole, so they end up well short of it, and miss the next putt. Just think of it this way: if you leave a chip or putt 8 feet short, it could have to traveled 15 more feet before you'd have a longer putt than you just gave yourself. That's giving you a lot of room to improve and get closer to the hole for your next putt. And regardless of speed, you also can't make a putt if you underestimate the amount of break to play. So if you resolve to miss every putt, inside of 15 feet, on the high side, you'll make more putts and lower your scores.

These two strategies: getting to the ball to the hole, and allowing for the putt to break more, is how the best players, like Jordan, make so many putts. I challenge you to adopt that strategy. Now, there will always be some shots that require circumspection, so don't be reckless, but if you have a routine chip or putt, then give the hole a chance to catch the ball, give the ball a chance to fall. You'll be surprised by the results.

The bunker hole-out got Jordan into a playoff with Zach Johnson and David Hearn. It was a long shootout, but the precocious and confident Spieth outlasted the two veterans. In that playoff, he crafted another miraculous shot from out of the trees on the 18th hole, a shot he spoke fondly of: *"on 18, our 5th hole [of the playoff], I punched a 7-iron out of the trees, kind of cut it off the water and ran it up to the back of the green, when the other two [Johnson and Hearn] were in trouble. And what's really interesting is a lot of focus ends up on the bunker shot of that tournament. But to me, I remember hitting that punch 7-iron, and now I'm thinking, 'Why was that such an easy shot for me then?' Like I'm sitting here going, 'Man like alright, just a little punch 7-iron, cut off the water, split the water and the bunker and run it up on the green.' Like I can see the shot. And it was just like, 'Oh yeah, I'll just hit the punch-cut 7-iron up the green.' And I'm sitting here now, like how is that [what] I was thinking there, and how do I get to where I can just think that way again? And it's just kind of funny. It just was so simple. It's just hit your normal punch shot."*

Simplicity of approach is truly a thing, and sometimes we do tend to overthink things. I have heard many a grizzled tour pro comment on a young golfer's audacious approach to some shots. The veteran's response is normally something like, "Give them a few years of failure and scar tissue, and I bet they won't try that again."

While the voice of experience is important, if a golfer is playing well, I'd always advocate going with their first instinct. If they don't have their best stuff, I would advise caution, but through it all, just like Jordan admitted, simple is the way to go. The fearlessness of youth is sometimes what's needed in a moment to pull off the remarkable.

I still wanted to poke Jordan a little more to try and

get the skinny on his skill around the greens, and how he holes so many shots at important times. It's a rare and uncanny ability: one that anyone on the planet would love to have. I remember, early in Spieth's pro career, I dubbed him the "American Seve," which is possibly the highest compliment I could pay a golfer. When I asked about his short game development, he explained, *"Part of it is just where I had to learn the short game—and I'll explain that in a second—and the other part is being advised by my instructor Cameron McCormick, [who said] chipping is not the full swing at all. You're doing completely different motions. You're changing full planes of motion depending on contact, certain lies, how quickly you need to stop it, where the ball is located: bunker, rough, fairway. They all could have completely different motions depending on what's presented. So the idea that you would practice something you're doing on your full swing is not correct, unless it's a basic shot from 30+ yards that you'd hit like you'd hit a full shot. And we just don't experience that much around the greens."* Skill and success around the greens are a function of imagination and creativity. All of the short-game experts exhibit those qualities as well as the mental liberty to think of those shots in terms of spin, speed, and trajectory. They aren't just trying to get the ball close, they're trying to make the ball perform in a certain fashion that will propel it toward the target in a desired manner.

I view short-game shots like tennis or ping-pong shots. They're created by using the racquet or paddle in various ways, speeds, and angles to get different types of speeds and spins. In the interest of keeping it simple, a lob shot in golf is similar to a drop shot in tennis, and a chip-and-run shot is akin to a little top-spin volley. The draw spin, similar to top spin, guarantees the ball would roll out and not check on the first bounce or two. Don't forget about the role of spin in the roll of the ball.

In other words, when you practice, once you have

any sort of strike consistency, focus on how you are spinning the ball with your clubface. In many ways, that clubface acts just like a tennis racquet or a ping-pong paddle. Jordan continued, and I was hanging on his every word: *"And so growing up at Brookhaven Country Club, which has a great facility now, but when I was learning the game, their short-game area consisted of one bunker, some rough, and a very, very firm, fast, small sloping AstroTurf green. So it was turf, and so I had to learn how to spin the ball incredibly just to keep it on this chipping green, as well as learning how to hit shots really high out of the rough, being okay with putting speed under the ball with a lot of loft. Honestly, it was just very hard to keep it on the green that I learned how to practice on. And so I learned how to play bunker shots hitting very close to the ball, and that's how I still do it to this day.*

As I listened to Jordan, I was reminded of how much of a difference the turf you learned to play on affects your approach to the short game. I saw this many times during my time as a college golf coach in Columbus, Georgia. As a South African, I had a natural "in" with South African kids, so I recruited a few of them. They all made a significant impact to our program, but they all struggled with chipping and pitching the ball when they arrived onto the Bermuda grass of the southeast U.S. South Africans are used to chipping and pitching off Kikuyu grass, and there's a sharp contrast between Kikuyu and Bermuda. Kikuyu has a strong, thick blade that perches the ball up and allows for more of a picking or sweeping chipping and pitching action. The Bermuda grass of the Southeast is a thinner blade, and the golf ball tends to "sit down" on its surface. This lie requires a completely different action through impact, as the ball needs to be compressed and dug out of the lie a bit more. As it pertains to Jordan Spieth, the firm practice green and the Bermuda grass in Dallas taught him to develop a technique that allowed him to spin and stop the ball quickly: a true case of necessity being the mother of invention.

Derek Ingram, the head golf coach for Golf Canada told me that Adam Hadwin and Nick Taylor—both PGA Tour winners—are tremendous chippers and pitchers of the ball, given the environment in which they learned the game. Both Canadians grew up on the west coast of Canada, where conditions tend to be damp and wet: conditions in which the ball tends to sit down in the fairway. Those lies promote a more descending strike for better results. Hence, with sharper, more downward angles of attack, both Taylor and Hadwin are great chippers whose downward technique fits with what is required on Bermuda.

The lesson behind the anecdote: sometimes it's not you that is the failure ... it could just be the conditions that are different than your norm. And all that is required are one or two marginal adjustments to modify the strike on the ball. When my boys who grew up in South Africa on Kikuyu grass learned at Columbus State the variances required for consistent contact off a different grass surfaces and got accustomed to the changes, they quickly adapted and became successful, and this ability to adapt to different turf made them more complete and well-rounded players.

Spieth continued as he described to me that his 60-degree wedge, to this day, has *"almost no bounce"* on the sole of the club, because it supports his approach to greenside shots: an approach or swing style he calls a "cover cut." There's another lesson in his insight: Get fitted for clubs, and don't be hesitant to modify your equipment to make you better. The investment will be well worth your while. And remember, when being fit for clubs, it's important that the fitting makes your bad shots better. Most people just pay attention to top-end information, like how their max spin or speed improves. I want every fitted club to help you on bad days, and I don't want you to have to modify how you swing to get the most out of it. If you're struggling with particular short-game shots, consider trying wedges with more or less bounce, or a different lie angle, and see if they better fit your most common short-game techniques.

With that said, a lob wedge with *very* low bounce is not common, even among tour pros with very skilled hands. But Jordan is crazy good, and he knows what works for him. With that low-bounce wedge, Jordan's sole focus is where the leading edge of the club collides with the grass, ground, or sand. Spieth explains, *"Regardless if I'm controlling my entry point, and my entry point remains consistent, now I have distance control regardless of the sand."* This point about entry point in the sand is key for amateur golfers to understand, as it may affect the outcome of all of your bunker shots around the greens more than anything. A simple drill to improve your entry point is to make a long line in the sand and that runs down between and in the middle of your feet. See where the line falls between your feet, and then make a swing, and strive to land the club on the line in the sand, and make an impression in the sand that points toward the target.

It's not as easy as it sounds, but practice it until you can consistently land the club on the line as you swing through to a full finish. Once you achieve consistency, put a golf ball on the target side of the line, only about an inch in front of the line. Make a swing that strikes the line and follows through to a finish. Strive to "throw" the "cushion" of sand you strike onto the green, and you'll see how it propels the ball out of the bunker and onto the green. Do that, and you're studying where your club enters the sand. When you're able to predict and control that entry point, relative to the ball, then even you'll be able to hit bunker shots like Jordan Spieth.

As it relates to pitching the ball, Jordan did caution

golfers against trying his cover-cut action, but he did say it would allow any golfer to be more aggressive. He does make a great point about taking advice from top pros: there are no secret moves, and it will take a lot of hard work to develop the skills to accomplish what they're asking you to do. He says, *"It's incredibly hard for me to give any advice to anybody in a pro-am, because unless you go do it, and just get comfortable doing it. What I mean by that is that cover-cut motion—that you're going to hit ball first and you're going to take a divot even if it's a 10-yard shot—you're gonna go ahead and be aggressive into the ball."* Don't try this out during a round: it'll take a lot of earnest practice to have that kind of consistent contact. As he described his cover-cut motion a little more, he touched on the fact that too many golfers try to lob the ball high in order to stop it fast. Jordan advises the opposite approach: a lower trajectory, but with spin. He explained how he does it on pitch shots: *"So I try to make up for it [lack of height] with spin, by hitting ball first and being very aggressive into the ground. And then the cutting motion allows me to make sure that my swing direction is significantly to the left, making it a little bit easier to make sure I'm hitting ball first. I can open the face up, the club still sits with very little bounce behind the ball, that either can allow for a little more height, a little more spin, or both— so I have that option. But there's a lot of times you just have to accept the fact that you can't lift it up in the air when you're chipping. And once you get comfortable being more aggressive than you want to be into the ball, really from any surface, any lie, it actually makes chipping quite a bit easier. But you have to almost get uncomfortable to be comfortable, if that makes sense. You just got to do it enough to start to believe in it."*

That's a huge takeaway, and one that connects Jordan's many successes under extreme pressure, and his ability to pull off great short shots: *"You have to almost get uncomfortable to be comfortable ... you just got to do it enough to start to believe in it."* Growth doesn't occur without trying, without stepping outside your comfort zone, without learning and perfecting new shots and techniques. It's unlikely you'll ever trust those new shots and techniques if you don't test them in uncomfortable situations.

Beyond his grit, determination, and otherworldly short game, Jordan Spieth is also a tremendously cerebral young man with a mental approach that's truly on the mark. He illustrated this when we discussed his Masters triumph in 2015. I asked him if it was the best golf he had ever played, and he countered with a lesson he learned in the 2014 Masters, the year before. He replied, *"It was just a continuation of tightening things up from what was already really good the previous two weeks, and regardless of where I was going to be at, and I just tried to use the year before [2014] as a learning tool. I needed a little more patience on Sunday. I needed to hole a few more putts. I had a few decent looks against Bubba that could've put the pressure on at 14, and that I missed on the par fives. And I thought, 'Keep your head down, because just because you had the lead through seven or eight holes on Sunday at Augusta doesn't mean you won't lose it by #10,' which is what happened in 2014."* There's that word *patience* again. It just seems to pop up everywhere when a great player talks about playing good golf. He continued as he talked about being present and not looking ahead or behind over the final nine holes: *"And so that just kind of kept me, I think, very patient that year to continue it into the back nine. To not even think that anything, that's not looking ahead until I got to really 17 green. 16 [green] I made a big putt to avoid a two-shot swing with Justin Rose."* He remained patient and in the moment, just focusing on the next shot he had.

He won that 2015 Masters in record fashion, and he

followed it up with three more victories, including a U.S. Open and the Tour Championship, and was crowned the FedEx Cup Champion and the PGA Tour Player of the Year. He ended 2015 ranked #1 in the world, at the age of 22. His triumphal march continued into 2016, and it seemed like whenever he teed it up, he was going to be in contention.

He reached a crescendo in July 2017, with a barnstorming win in the Open Championship. Jordan put his incisive and acute mental skill on display when he recounted his battle with Matt Kuchar in the final round at Royal Birkdale. Among other things, he talked about the scrambling save after a wild tee-shot on the 13th hole. Then he dropped the golden nugget, one that every sports psychologist would reference, that allowed a look inside Jordan's mind, his competitive mindset, and his uplifting self-talk: *"I actually was walking to the next hole, and I lost the lead with five to go, and I remember going to use restroom in the Port-O-Let, and I remember actually being in there and being like 'alright, you lost it [the lead], but you're only down one. There's nobody else around. It's just him that you're playing against. And you can beat him by two shots on these last five holes.'"*

Spieth called that five-hole stretch of golf some of the best golf he had ever played. Isn't that switch incredible, given he had just blown a tee-shot miles right on the 13th hole? There is indeed power in positive self-talk. He elaborated further: *"My confidence level, my game was not thrown off by one tee shot that I hit. It was [thinking], I'm playing really well; it started raining a little, and I made a mistake not committing to a shot, caught a little water ball. This is what I'm telling myself in my head ... whether it's true or not doesn't matter. Let's step up and hit an iron shot and just try to have a putt to win each hole. And I remember thinking about that all while I'm in there, and I stepped out of there and I probably hit the best shot I would say that I've ever hit.*

To this day, it was a 6-iron I hit on 14. Once I won that hole, I said 'I got this guy,' and the rest is history." It truly was meant to be, perhaps manifested in Jordan's mind. His manner, mindset, and self-talk are things that I challenge my lesson-takers—no matter their skill level—to strive toward. Ask yourself, What are you manifesting with your mouth? With your mind? Do an inventory of the things you say and think. Chances are, what you say and think are what you believe, and that will fuel what comes next for you. Hopefully you'll realize that you're doing exactly the opposite of what the ultimate competitor does.

I will remind you of something that you likely glossed over in Jordan's comment: *"This is what I'm telling myself in my head; whether it's true or not, doesn't matter."* So go ahead and talk yourself up. Be your own best friend. Speak life into your game. Faith comes by hearing. So like Spieth, speak it, manifest it. Sow the seeds for success, not failure. Don't scuttle all of your good work with self-deprecating drivel.

I got excited when Jordan got into his competitive self-analysis, and I compared him to Tom Brady under pressure. Both Spieth and Brady get a look in their eye, and you can see them drop into a different, more intense and focused manner. Spieth didn't defer or play it off; instead, he delved further: *"Every experience helps you kind of create those perspectives. You know, stuff's gonna happen. Stuff can happen. It can be clean. But when stuff happens, what's the point in dragging it on if you still have more holes left?"* Take a minute and consider how many times you've dragged stuff on in a round, that stuff that happens no matter how well you're playing. That stuff is unnecessary baggage that really is of no use to you. It's not productive or helpful. Offload that which is weighing you down. I don't care what it is. It could be that bad bounce, or that double bogey. It could even be a quadruple bogey, like Spieth made on the 12th in the 2016 Masters. Let it go! If you don't, you already know the outcome.

Always look forward to the next shot, and what you can achieve with that shot through a positive mindset. Jordan told this relatable story from the final round of the 2016 Masters: *"I got to 13 tee, and Smiley Kaufman will tell you—he made a 2 and I made a 7 [on the par-three 12th]—and we got to the tee and I said, 'Whose tee is it, Smiley?' And he was shocked; he had no idea what to even say. And my point in saying this is, look: 'I mean, it happens. You know I have six holes left. I can play them a few under and have a chance to win. I think I played them in two [under] maybe. And I did have a chance to win.'"* Here's a guarantee. Stuff is going to happen in every round you play. Deal with it, or as my mother would say: "Get over it and get on with it." Sometimes, a little humor can go a long way toward putting a bad hole behind you. Keep your wits and your confidence up: every hole is a new hole.

Here's Jordan's advice: *"I have experienced stuff like that where it's like, look stuff happened. What are you going to do? You still have golf left, so you may as well be trying to hit every shot where you're looking, and every putt where you're looking. Just like [I] tried to before when it didn't work out, but doesn't mean it won't now."* The best competitors have a way of bouncing back, as Spieth has done many times. Create this mindset when you have a bad hole, and you'll possess a bullet-proof mental game for competition.

No one in this book will say they play their best with a negative mindset. It's just not possible. As the great Bobby Jones once said, "The main idea in golf as in life, I suppose is to learn to accept what cannot be altered and to keep on doing one's own reasoned and resolute best whether the prospect be bleak or rosy." In other words, focus and presence of mind are absolutes, no matter what is going on. Spieth had just made a 7 on the par-three 12th and had pretty much drowned his chances of winning the Masters, yet he still kept his focus and his never-say-die attitude. As Winston Churchill famously said, "never give in. Never, never, never, never—in nothing, great or small, large or petty—never give in, except to convictions of honor and good sense. Never yield to force. Never yield to the apparently overwhelming might of the enemy."

In golf, you *are* going to get knocked down. But keep getting up. Fall down seven times, get up eight is pretty much a common denominator with every great golfer I've encountered. Jordan exhibited this attitude, and mindset, when his game fell into a slump. Jordan remembers, *"I struggled for a couple of years, and I actually really learned what it was like to get out of a kind of ego-driven golf and into kind of mastery-driven golf, and what that meant, how to define that, and how to work that into my life and golf."* Ego-driven golf is something we *all* fall prey to, whether it be a stupid decision on the course or an unwarranted or unmerited expectation that leads to a misstep somehow. Thinking you can pull something off just because you have before is the start of a good process, not the end. You still have to focus and execute every shot. That's where mastery comes in. The golf ball doesn't know who you are, what you normally shoot, how many matches or tournaments you've won (or lost). Mastery-driven golf is where true and lasting success resides, where a golfer is more enchanted with—and attentive to—the execution of the stroke instead of the result or the reward from good playing. In my opinion, a mastery-driven approach also mitigates the pressure on a player, because, remember, stuff happens in golf: bad bounces, poor lies, and balls coming to rest in a divot. It's just how golf is, and self-pity will get you nowhere.

Jordan Spieth seems to have learned this perspective through the times when he didn't have his best golf. He recalls, *"I felt like the bigger the moment, the bigger the potential to go one way, I kind of was able to always calm myself down: the uncomfortable, get more comfortable in a weird way. And it worked once, it didn't work another time, and I've had plenty of times in between. You know, it's just the game. Sometimes I'll play really really well and on the back end of something it doesn't work out, and sometimes I'll play a little less good and I win. It just depends on how the other guys around did."* Golf is fickle. It isn't easy, and often the challenge is more mental than it is physical. I have seen countless golfers grind on the range or the putting green in an effort to regain form, but the truth is there's more to it than just improving technique. And rest assured, you are not the only golfer who has been in that horrible place where it seems almost impossible to hit the ball squarely and on line when it really matters. Trust me, even Tiger Woods and Jack Nicklaus have struggled at one stage or another.

Every golfer I know has been driven to despair by our wonderful game. But the good news is that the tide does turn. And it turns because you remain true to who you are and the complete effort you're giving. Jordan focuses on mastery-driven golf—executing great golf shots, one at a time, again and again—and lets the chips fall as they may. When you have that focus on execution, good results are bound to happen. He remembered how this mentality got him through some tough times: *"I missed the cut, still playing poorly in 2021 at San Diego. And that was probably rock bottom for me. You know, I had tears. I didn't know. It's just another start to another season. I know I'm trying to do the right things now. Taking control mentally, talking to people, putting in some work to try and help get out of fight-or-flight [response], to do some breathing, to introduce some of that meditation stuff. And it just was like 'man, I'm looking to get off to a good start and I just didn't.'"* When it's not going your way, just admit that it's not going your way, and keep going. Stay patient, stay true to you, stay focused on the process of improvement. Stay focused on excecution or mastery. If you do, a positive change in form is sometimes closer than you think. Jordan's shift happened the following week. *"By the by, the Saturday of the next week, I shot 61, and I was in the final group in Phoenix."* As you can see, if you just keep working with focus and intent, the results can follow, and the momentum can swing back in the blink of any eye.

Speaking of swings, lots of great players have had highly unique swings. The important thing was that it worked for them, delivering the clubfact to the ball appropriately and consistently. Jordan talked about going through some swing changes and the temptation to go back to previous swings. He referenced conversations with Jason Dufner to that end. Focusing on what your swing looks like is ego-driven golf; focusing on what your swing does to the ball is mastery-driven golf. Jordan cautions, *"don't even worry about it [the swing] looking this way. It doesn't matter. As long as you're doing this into impact, and it feels like this at impact, then you're going to be in a better place. You know, I was always so video obsessed for a few years. Why does this not look like it does here? I'm trying this, I'm trying that. How can I not match up to any degree to what it looked like in 2015, or 2017, or 2013, whatever. And that got me out of that. So it got me impact-focused, ball-flight focused."* The practice of cookie-cutter instruction— that SonyCam era I talked about in the Introduction— should be long gone. It simply doesn't work. Know your swing, and swing your swing. And as it changes over time—and I will guarantee that everyone's swing changes over time—keep looking forward, not back.

The swing critic—either the ones out there offering unsolicited advice, or the one that resides in all of our heads—can be an awfully difficult boss to appease. If things aren't perfect, the swing critic will jump on that imperfection. If you keep listening to the critics—especially the one inside you—you won't ever progress. Focus on the execution of the stroke and keep your eyes on your own lane. And when those good results come, the voice of the swing critic will go away. Jordan has learned to play for himself and not in order to appease the critic. When I asked him what he would one day teach his kids, or put in his memoirs, he responded: *"It's not the critic who counts."*

I started the chapter by mentioning that, when his career is complete, Jordan Spieth may be the competitive equal to Seve Ballesteros. The truth is that with a PGA Championship victory, Spieth would complete another exceptionally rare milestone for any golfer: the career grand slam. The fraternity of players to achieve this feat is small and illustrious: Jack Nicklaus, Tiger Woods, Bobby Jones, Gene Sarazen, Gary Player, and Ben Hogan. That's a club of only six names, and they're arguably six of the seven biggest names in the past 100 years of competitive golf history. And you thought having a green jacket was a rare club to be in! They all had their own swings; swings that changed over their careers, too.

Here's the thing. Jordan Spieth is that good: both mentally and physically. The critic is gone, and the belief is there. Not driven by ego, he seeks mastery. And now he has all the experiences—good and bad—to get him through the rest. Through it all, he's gotten comfortable with being uncomfortable. And that should make his competitors *very* uncomfortable.

Really great golf is played first in the mind because action follows thought.

Dr. Bob Winters

5

Bob Winters

Purposeful Intent and Vested Indifference

Whenever I can, I always make time to talk to Dr. Bob Winters, and whenever I do, I always learn something. Something that—with his permission—I hope to pass on to golfers in need.

Winters' friendly and approachable nature belie his fierce intellect. He truly has a teacher's heart, and no matter the situation, he is most comfortable dispensing wisdom and insight to golfers of all skill levels. It's just who he is and what he does.

Winters is a former assistant golf coach at the University of Virginia and serves as the resident sports psychologist at the Leadbetter World Teaching Headquarters at ChampionsGate outside of Orlando. Bob earned a PhD in sports psychology from UVA and has been mentored by some of the finest minds in the field, including Dr. Linda Bunker and the original Dr.

Bob: Bob Rotella. He has coupled his insights on performance enhancement and confidence development with his competitive knowledge of the game to become a published author and a confidant and counsel to the pros.

His insights and his caring manner are two of the many reasons why I've featured him more than once on my *On the Mark* podcast. Dr. Bob is highly quotable and has dropped countless nuggets on me that I'll long remember. *"Goals should be stepping stones, not stopping stones to success,"* and *"Goals are dreams with a deadline"* are two that a lodged at the forefront of my mind. Respectfully Dr. Bob gives credit to his friend Dr. Dan Gould of Greensboro, North Carolina for the first quotation. Gould was speaking of not exceeding your competencies and making the goals too high: a strategy likely to lead to failed attempts and eventual disappointment.

Here is Winters' thought on it, while updating the metaphor: *"Taking a step or two further with that thought, I imagined the concept of baby steps to success. That is, if you understand that the risers in a set of stairs [or a ladder] are too high, or that it is unlikely to assist in your ability to move up the stairs, then the riser itself is too high, and you may become fatigued, injured, or just not want to get to the next level. The ability to stay committed to your motivation to continue will be seriously hampered."* With goal setting being an important part of self-development and measurement, it's important to set appropriate, achievable, and measurable goals. Goals should be a stretch, but achievable at whatever stage you are. Dr. Winters continues: *"the same is true in setting goals for yourself in golf. If you set the goal too high, you will become frustrated and you will lose intrinsic motivation to continue. If one relates this to golf, the common advice of playing one shot at a time is simply the notion of taking it one doable step at a time versus trying to shoot a certain score or win a tournament all at once!"* Our minds like to think ahead—often very far ahead— but the work is in staying present and not losing focus on the purpose and goal of the now.

His second quotation, that I often recycle to aspi- rant golfers and competitors—*"Goals are dreams with a deadline"*—blends the beauty of dreams with the re- ality of the aspect of time. When you add the aspect of time, it helps to you to focus on what you need to do to- day to reach that goal down the road. Winters relates these ideas to goal-setting theories in psychology: *"This is a cliché that has been around for a long time, but the way I make sense of it is that, when we think of S.M.A.R.T. Goals—Specific, Measurable, Attainable, Realistic, and Time-Constrained—what we are saying is that each goal you set for yourself should be achievable, within certain human limits. Anything that is unattainable or simply be- yond the scope of your time and resources may not be a goal at all, but simply a whimsical want or desire that hasn't been fully thought through to its completion."* For example, instead of saying you want to become a 5- or 10-handicap, which is too vague with no guidance, set the goal to shave, say, 4 strokes off your average score in 6 months, by focusing on lowering your average num- ber of putts by 2 strokes and limiting yourself to 1 dou- ble bogey per round. Now that's S.M.A.R.T.

The normally congenial Dr. Bob delivers a bit of a gut punch there. He continued: *"Having said that, grit is the persistence to go after a long-term goal, and this is where there is a fine curtain between being realistic or going after the possible, which to many seems impos- sible or incredulous to think that this may or may not happen for you."* Through S.M.A.R.T. goal setting, you're more likely to reach your goals, and reaching your ini- tial goals will develop confidence and make you hun- grier to achieve your next goals. In doing so, you're cul- tivating a capacity for grit.

If I stopped the chapter at this point to allow you to meditate on those two gems, you'd likely find that as you unpack either of them, they are sure to help you to better golf. I do however need to get to three of Bob Winters' "7 Keys to Playing Great Golf." (You can hear the other four on the podcast episode.)

Winters tees us up with his inspiration for his 7 Keys: *"I thought to myself, before I leave this great golf course called Planet Earth and move on, I really would like to have this magnum opus. I would really like to have a body of work ... about what it means to really play your game. What does it mean to beat the golf course? What does it mean to play one shot at a time? Because that is the foundation that has been working for the Ben Hogans, the Jack Nicklauses, the Tigers, and the Annika Sorenstams."* Winters is adamant that players believe that they are competing against the golf course, not directly with other golfers. You don't worry about what other players are doing, or what they're capable of, or their record or reputation. If you are thinking about your competitors' great abilities or reputation, you are already on your way to losing. You must focus on what you can do and have the confidence that you've done the work before the competition. Then, you should let yourself *play*.

Dr. Winters' keys can be applied by every golfer, and I think they can stand the test of time. He stated that a golfer could apply and use just one or more of them and improve as they are based on *"possibility thinking and purposeful doing"* and not on just being positive. Winters explains, *"The first key to playing great golf, for all people, is this simple little foundation key. It's: 'I play my game.' And it's my game. I work on it, I develop it, I take ownership of that game, and I play to please the team that I call Team Me. ... But that team isn't your coach, it isn't your parents, it isn't in your girlfriend, spouse, husband or wife, aunt or uncle: it's made of three great beings: and that is me, myself, and I. That is Team You.*" I love this observation, as I was one of those golfers who always played and competed with a concern for what others would think. Now, over 30 years removed from competition, I have the benefit of hindsight, and I've realized that approach severely handcuffed me and kept me from playing free, with no abandon, to allow my best to shine. Comparing your game to others' is not only counter-productive, it's detrimental.

Dr. Bob built on the acronym P.L.A.Y.: *"I've always loved the word,* play. *P.L.A.Y. means to Perform Like A Youth. To have this youthful innocence, to have this naïveté to go out and play. Because what happens is that golfers, just by their very nature, work super hard, and they're trying very hard. And they're putting in a lot of sweat equity—every day—into getting better. And they put so much seriousness into their practice. And then the paradox is we're supposed to go out and free it up and play as if it doesn't mean anything. As if it doesn't [matter]. And so there's this paradoxical intention there. The point of it is that when you play your game, you have to develop a personal playing philosophy that is consistent with how you see, feel, and believe in things."* In other words, you have to be comfortable in your own skin and in the way you play the game. After all, if Tiger Woods tried to play like somebody else, he may not ever have fulfilled his potential.

When I chat with Bob Winters, our conversations always venture down rabbit holes, and we spent a lot of time unpacking mental concepts before we got to the next key: *"Beat the Course. The Course is Your True Opponent."* Winters expanded on this idea: *"I'm always telling my people and my students, you might have 144 people in this field, your task isn't to beat the 143 other players. Your task is to play your A-game and to beat the golf course. The golf course is your opponent. I think we all come in this whole vein of playing on team sports, and my team versus your team: it's me versus you. We call it* direct competition. *I win by making you lose, or vice versa. But in golf, it's a* parallel competition. *That is, we're all playing, we're all teeing off the same time. And what's the performance arena? It's the golf course. So in* parallel competition, *I'm doing my thing, you're doing your thing; everybody else is doing their thing. But the true opponent is the golf course. And it's just sitting there waiting for us."* If you approach competition this way, you'll be focused on what you're capable of—the best you can do—rather than reacting to whatever someone else is doing.

We can spend a lot of time measuring ourselves against others, and that takes us off track. The golf course is the exam, and you should just keep your eyes on your own test, because you should think you're the best in the room. A test is not human, and neither is the golf course, and this is an advantage: it's safe to look right at your competitor and take it on. As Bob says, the course *"doesn't care about your feelings, good, bad, or indifferent."* Speaking of not caring, your competitors don't either. The best ones are just focused on their own game.

As a young competitor-golfer, I learned the following lesson from a wily old pro. To make a long story short, the lesson basically goes that if you shoot 75, half of your competitors are happy you shot 75, the other half of your competitors are wishing you had shot 76 or worse. So in other words, get over the bad day and get on with it. Stop crying over the spilled milk. If you didn't win, no one cares what you shot.

As far as scores go, Dr. Winters made the following point: *"You first have to realize the most valuable number in golf. And that is not par 72. It's not 68. It's not 54. The most valuable number in golf is 1, the number 1, because [there's only one] shot in the world at any one moment you can do anything about."* That observation leads us into another of Winters' keys: "Play One Shot at a Time." This takes a lot of intention. Bob shares the mentality of a focused, purposeful shot: *I make a clear and purposeful plan on each shot I hit! I become clear of my intention. I think every person needs to understand that when you make a clear and purposeful plan, long before you step in to hit the golf shot, that's really where great golf is played: in your decision making behind the ball.*" This is the mindset where thinking is clear, concise, focused, and full of intent. The mindset is the genesis of every golf shot, and commitment leads to better execution.

Bob Winters also continually preaches the importance of a clear mind. In his words, *"clarity equals confidence."* If I may, I'd add that it also promotes competence. If anyone would approach every shot with clear intent and a complete idea of the swing move ... that golfer would begin to find the golf swing becoming more streamlined, smooth, uninterrupted and—as a result—successful. Bob adds, *"That's really what trusting your swing and really having confidence is all about. I know what to do. I've seen the shot, I've really created a nice rehearsal, and now I've committed to it. So here we go. And so that's why I think clarity equals confidence."*

Clarity and having a clear and purposed plan before every shot also goes a long way to mitigating doubt. And as I wholeheartedly maintain, doubt is one of the biggest wreckers of the golf swing.

Dr. Winters believes this too. As a matter of fact, he thinks doubt is the top reason for failure and shortcoming: *"your own self-doubt is your number one performance interference."* And he advises and teaches that self-doubt and confidence are like two weights on a scale of justice. Hence, as confidence improves, self-doubt diminishes.

This is the perfect segue to pivot to two Bob Winters theories that have resonated with me and have made me a better teacher and coach: *"purposeful intent" and "vested indifference."* The first time Dr. Bob mentioned these concepts to me, my mind immediately went to a tip that Gary Player once shared with me. Mr. Player advised that I should "hit every shot as if it was the last shot I would ever hit." That is purposeful intent.

At the time the advice sounded trite, but the more I considered it the more it occurred to me that the approach is exactly the one adopted by nearly every top performer. Think about it for a minute: if you were only allowed to hit one more shot, for the rest of your life, you'd surely ensure you are ready for it. Let me put in another way: you are standing on the tee of a par three, and if you make a hole-in-one you get a million dollars. Surely you would ensure you get the correct yardage and calculate the wind speed and direction. You'd make a practice swing or two. You'd likely visualize the shot and adopt a good, positive attitude and mindset. You'd most certainly ensure that fundamentals like alignment and ball position are on point and correct. Finally you'd probably make a smooth, unhurried, purpose-filled golf swing. After all, there is a chance to win a million bucks!

That very approach of getting your mind and body in the right place for the shot, that care, that purpose, that attention to detail, that optimistic mindset, that hope for success: these all make up purposeful intent, and every shot deserves that from you.

Let me remind you of something you already know: every shot has exactly the same value. Whether it's a two-foot putt or a 300-yard drive, its value is 1. Hence, it would make sense that every shot deserved the same amount of attention, right? To be realistic, I'm fully aware that certain shots just seem more important than others. The point I am trying to make is that, if you want to be consistently successful, you *have to* avoid the bad attitudes, the negative self-talk, the lack of focus, and often the disregard for rudimentary elements such as accommodations for wind, elevation, and the true distance the ball is traveling.

Every successful professional covers every single one of the bases before he or she hits a shot. Or as Dr. Winters says, *"Expect of yourself that you're going to commit yourself to every shot, as purposefully as you possibly can."* Now if elite golfers—with their copious skills and high talent levels—do so, then surely you should too.

Purposeful intent: it's not necessarily a guarantee for instant low scores. It will however guarantee that over the long haul, those horrid shots—the ones that turn into big numbers—will begin to dissipate. And if you manage to arrive at that place, you'll discover the ability to navigate around the bad days with limited damage to the scorecard.

On the other side of the coin is *vested indifference:* it occurs when a person takes personal ownership of an attitude that has a complete lack of regard or concern for any results. Being indifferent to results is an awfully hard mental state to achieve, but its reward is incredibly liberating, both mentally and emotionally. In my experience, a lack of concern for results allows a golfer the freedom to make unencumbered, free-flowing swings. Rory McIlroy, with a driver in his hand is perhaps the best personification of vested indifference. When he swings the driver, it appears that he is in balance, but swinging the club at maximum speed. There is never any holding back for fear of failure.

I mentioned earlier that doubt wrecks golf swings. More specifically, doubt and fear typically result in tension, and tension is like a wrecking ball for a golf swing.

By definition, a swing is a free-flowing, rhythmic mechanism that is only guided by the connection point to which it is attached. If this point is locked down, the swing of the apparatus connected to it will cease to exist.

The principle most certainly holds true in the golf swing. Add any tension, or an environment where the freedom of the swing is scuttled or encumbered, the chances of success are diminished. Tension has a few origins, but it is largely born out of fear, apprehension, or concern.

Do you see where I am going here? If you earnestly heed Dr. Winters' advice, you'll be able to get to a place—with your mind and your body—where you are focused, positive, optimistic, purposeful before the shot: purposeful intent.

Then when you're over the ball and ready to go, you relax and swing the club with scant regard for the result, because your only concern is to do the very best, in your *current* situation with your *current* ability and skill set: vested indifference.

The swing that's about to happen has nothing to do with your potential, or how you have been playing, or your historical resume, or your expectations. That swing is a stitch in time and a single part of a long story.

I have heard it said by many an elite golfer that they strive to make aggressive swings toward conservative targets. Most of us however pick targets that are outside of our realistic skill level and then deep down, because our subconscious registers that we really aren't capable of pulling of the shot consistently, we become apprehensive, even fearful and we make an unconvinced, defensive golf swing.

Sadly, all too often the result is negative, and that becomes a mental building block for more doubtful, tension-ridden swings.

Good shots most certainly originate in your mind. Let that settle in your soul. Realize that galvanizing your mental approach will do your game as many favors as what practicing will. As Bob Winters so wisely signed off by saying, *"For me, the very best expectation to have is the expectancy that you're going to go out, and you're going to give yourself permission—emotional freedom so to speak—to play your game the very best way you can. And to expect of yourself that you're going to commit yourself to every shot, as purposefully as you possibly can ... and also to be able to accept that whatever happens. I can live with it, because I stepped into that shot giving it my best."*

So I learned an awful lot from [Seve Ballesteros]: playing practice rounds, playing in tournaments with him, and also watching him on the practice tee, and also around the chipping area. ... We'd have 50 or 60 shots out of a bunker. And of course, we'd be playing $1 shot, and I'd lose 25 bucks, because he'd beat me almost every [shot], but I learned! It was probably the best $25 I ever invested.

Nick Price

6

Nick Price

A Bad Day Decent

As one of the southern hemisphere's greatest ever—a multiple major champion, hall-of-famer, and former World #1 golfer—Nick Price is one of my favorite golfers of all time. I'm grateful to know him and even more grateful to call him a mentor and a friend.

Nick is one of the foremost ball-strikers of all time. His staccato, beautifully planed swing is one I always refer to. As a young golfer, I actually tried to copy his action. I quickly found out that Nick's natural rhythm and tempo is a lot faster than mine. My natural rhythm was always a bit easier, and when I tried to speed it up—to look like Nick Price—things didn't work very well. On the flipside, I suspect that if Nick tried to go at my slower speed, he may not have ended up a legend. That lesson on natural tempo is the first one I learned from him (albeit indirectly): always match your swing tempo and putting stroke cadence with your body and natural manner.

Nick Price is eloquent, generous, and wise. He's a fascinating listen, always willing to pass on the insight and expertise he has garnered in over 40 years of professional golf. I'll always make time to talk to Nick, and I was so happy when he agreed to come on the podcast. We started by talking about Nick's origins with the game. Just like many of us, he grew up dreaming of winning major tournaments. Born and raised in Rhodesia (now Zimbabwe), he wasn't necessarily exposed to much golf on television. In fact, the only golf he ever got to watch was on 16-mm promotional films. He spoke fondly of watching his first Open Championship: *"The first one I saw was 1969, which was at [Royal] Lytham [and St Annes], when Tony Jacklin won. I was 12 years old at the time. That was my first exposure to what a major championship looked like."* Young Nick fell in love with the Open Championship and was hooked: *"From an early age, when we were making those four-footers in the backyard, or wherever [we'd imagine], 'Hey, this is for the British Open.'"*

Here's where I want to challenge you to dream. Even if you aren't a kid anymore, you should still dream, and let those dreams motivate you to action. Go out and dream while practicing: make that putt to win the Masters, or the club championship, or to break 90 or 80 or par. Visualize and imagine these dreams happening in your mind. Putting yourself in that position is a great way to practice. Get those juices flowing. Go through your preshot routine. Create the environment in your mind and action it in practice. Dreaming creates possibilities. If you plant these seeds and they spur you to action, then I promise they'll germinate one day.

Now after hearing about Price's childhood dreaming, you'd imagine that he's always loved links golf and the Open. The funny thing, though, is that he had to learn that links golf requires a different approach altogether. Nick recalls, *"when I first played my first Open*

Championship—which was in 1975, as an amateur—I really wasn't a huge fan of links courses when I first played them. I spoke to Tom Watson at length one day ... about why this man from Kansas became one of the most prolific winners of the Open Championship. And [his initial impression of links golf was] the same as me. We joked about it. I said, 'Same as me, you know, when I first saw a links golf course, I didn't really like the way to play it.' But I guess over a period of time, you learn, and you learn to love the challenge of these great golf courses, which is so different to what so many of us are brought up playing." The great Bobby Jones felt that way about the Old Course at first, before becoming its greatest worldwide advocate. Remember that you shouldn't become frustrated by the course or style of golf, instead work toward understanding its nuances and your ability to adjust to it. When you do, you'll likely end up loving it.

Nick Price is open minded, and he has a curious mind, which helps him take on new challenges and adapt his game. I think that being curious is the best way to learn and keep learning. I am reminded of a bit of advice from the poet Walt Whitman: "Be curious, not judgmental." Curiosity may have killed the cat, but I'm convinced that it has healed many an ailing golfer. Now I'm not advocating that a golfer goes out and desperately tries any old swing tip in a vain attempt to improve their game. Instead, I'm saying that being open to learning is an attitude that—in my experience—is a common denominator to all high achievers.

As far as learning goes, Nick Price—and every great golfer—is a master tactician and strategist, with remarkable perspectives to share. As I mentioned, Nick always lavished advice and counsel to younger players, which he has learned from other greats—he has tremendous respect for Seve Ballesteros—and from his own experiences.

Personally, I've learned a heck of a lot from Nick, as

has my brother Trevor. Nick has also mentored other young South African players, notably major champions Charl Schwartzel and Louis Oosthuizen. He once shared this unique perspective on a four-day tournament to both young South Africans prior to a major: *"I've been saying to them ... if you look at a tournament on average, if a professional has a great ball-striking week, he's probably going to miss about 18 greens during that week. ... Three-to-four greens a day, [over] the four days, so call it 18 greens, and the guys who win are the guys who get it up and down 16 or 15 times out of those 18 times. Like Jordan Spieth does, like Jason Day does. So all these guys hit the ball much of a muchness [i.e., very similarly], and it's all about how many par saves the guys make, which really make your birdies count. So, once again, my advice: go and work on the short game."* It's an incredibly enlightening perspective, and one that can allow elite players to quickly forgive themselves for missing a few greens. And then motivate themselves to stay focused on getting up and down, and remain positive through the ups and downs. If even a preeminent ball-striker such as Nick is banking on missing three to four greens in regulation per round, then perhaps us mortal golfers should revisit our own expectations.

Nick is not only a fantastic ball-striker, he's also a great mental strategist. Through the years, Nick has recommended a few keys on strategy to me. In his book he listed a few of his keys:

- Always be yourself.
- When in doubt, play the shot that's the easiest for you to execute well.
- Let patience govern your mindset.
- Take a long-term approach to improvement.

And one last one, which Nick believes is essential to improvement and something he always writes in his yearly goal journals:

- Persevere, persevere, persevere.

Course management and self-management are crucial to good scoring. These also helped Nick win his most cherished major. Here's how.

Nick got better at competing on windy links courses—and on windy days elsewhere—by playing the percentages. Even though he's almost robotically accurate with any club in his hand, he's judicious with his decision-making, in order to hit more fairways and greens. As Nick explains, this is especially important in the wind: *"Anybody who's a good wind player doesn't fight it. You play for the wind. Now, obviously, on the odd occasion, there might be a pin that you may have to go to that's tucked on the right-hand side of the green, which means into right-to-left wind, you have to hit a cut to hold the ball on that wind, so that it doesn't get blown. But generally, no: don't fight the wind. Use it to your advantage, and even if there is a pin in the right-hand corner of a green and the wind's blowing from right to left, just accept it. You're going to hit the ball 25 to 30 feet away and take your chances. and along the way, there is going to be a pin on the left-hand side, or a pin to that you will have a chance to be aggressive. So I think in the wind, patience is a real virtue. Don't try to pressure yourself."* If Nick Price is respecting the wind, and not trying to manipulate it all the time, maybe we should too.

Price shared an interesting anecdote from his 1994 Open Championship win at Turnberry, about making the most out of what he had that day. It smacked of his key: *"Let patience govern your mindset."* Nick recounts, *"My ball striking hadn't been great on the Sunday. So I'd sort of played a little cautiously, because I wanted to stay in touch with the lead. And you know, when you're not hitting the ball exactly how you want to, or when you've got the odd, loose shot—which I definitely had on the practice tee that day—you don't want to plug it in the face of a bunker and take a double or a triple and knock yourself way out of the championship. So I played a little bit cautiously."*

I was surprised that someone who was contending for a major championship could be battling their ball striking, as I am sure you are. (Especially Nick, who has rarely missed the center of the clubface in decades.) But when I got over my surprise, what jumped out at me was how he modified his strategy based on his warm-up and played this round of links golf a little more safely. He was just trying to avoid disaster. That strategically cautious approach on the front nine kept Nick within reach of Jesper Parnevik, and it allowed him to play a little more aggressively down the stretch—when his ball-striking returned to its usual expert-level—to finally win his Open. Everyone has a bad stretch during 72 holes, but the winners minimize the damage. I often recount Nick Price's advice: *"I became a tournament-winner when I learned how to make my bad day decent."*

Remember that Price dreamed most of winning the Open, and after learning to play links golf effectively—using his cerebral and curious approach to adjustments—he would finish as runner-up twice before winning. One runner-up finish—to Seve Ballesteros in the 1998 Open at Royal Lytham and St. Annes—was a learning experience for him, and perhaps the catalyst to his major championship run a few years later: *"And I learned a huge lesson from him [Seve] that day, and that was: If I'm ever going to win a major championship, I'm going to have to work a lot harder on my short game. So I did."* In addition to working hard on his short game, Price later won the Open by also following all of his axioms I shared with you: be yourself, be curious and stay positive, play the percentages, use patience as your mindset, take a long-term approach to improvement, and persevere by making bad days decent.

To some degree, all of us desire what we don't have,

and Price is no different. He's always been a marvelous ball-striker, and by his own admission, his short game kept him from winning tournaments early in his career. So it's from his vast professional experiences that he says we should work on our scrambling, sand-game, pitching, and chipping to lower scores. Nick properly focused on his faults to improve his misses, and in doing so, he became a complete golfer and reached #1 in the world. Whatever the worst part of your game is, you need to focus on improving it, but as you do so, do not neglect your strengths.

One great way to get better at your worst skill is to watch the best at that skill. Nick talks a lot about learning from Seve: *"like so many guys of my age ... Faldo, myself, Langer ... all of us grew up really admiring Seve, because he at the age of 19 and 20 was streets ahead of us. We all were playing catch-up with Seve, because he could hit the shots, and his ability to get the ball up and down—in around the greens—was just unbelievable. I mean, what Seve did with a 56-degree wedge was absolute magic to watch. He was incredible. So I learned an awful lot from him: playing practice rounds, playing in tournaments with him, and also watching him on the practice tee, and also around the chipping area. And then a couple of times, we'd get in a bunker and we'd play closest [to the pin]. We'd have 50 or 60 shots out of a bunker. And of course, we'd be playing $1 shot, and I'd lose 25 bucks, because he'd beat me almost every [shot], but I learned! That was the big thing. It was probably the best $25 I ever invested."* If you can't beat 'em, you should learn from 'em.

In this story, I see a humble and curious mind: one that's open enough to learn from any place—even through willingly losing to a competitor—in order to improve. The important thing is being open to change. Nick sees some examples in the pro game today: *"When you look at Rory [McIlroy] and you look at Jason Day, and I love seeing these guys have now got driving irons back in the bag. Anytime you put the ball in the fairway more, you get a little more spin out the fairway with your iron shots, and the ball stops quicker, so you can be more aggressive. So that's a good thing."*

When Nick Price—one of the straightest drivers of his generation—tells you about the value of playing from the fairway, we should all listen. Now I recognize that tour strokes-gained metrics illustrate an advantage in hitting it as far as possible off the tee, and that some players these days can survive (and even thrive) using a bomb-and-gouge strategy. But this is only because the PGA Tour pro, thanks to his strength—and maybe some better technology with the ball and the club—is able to gouge a ball out of the rough and hit it high enough and with enough spin to have it land and stay on the green. In contrast, most mere mortals aren't strong enough, or fast enough, or accurate enough to extricate the ball from the rough well enough to use this strategy. For this reason, it's much more advantageous for the rest of us to play from the fairway. I'd take a drive 250 yards in the fairway rather than a longer shot, in the rough.

Finally, to score better, the simplest way to lower scores is by eliminating double bogeys and worse. A great way to do that is by reducing the number of tee shots that go in heavy rough, in the woods, or out of play. I've seen countless players litter golf courses with errant tee shots that are a result of trying to hit the ball too hard and too far. In contrast, I've rarely seen a ball in a fairway that compromises one's chances on the next shot.

Notice that Nick—despite his abilities with an iron in his hand—adopted a somewhat defensive attitude when it came to attacking flags and hole locations. It's not playing scared or tentative: it's playing smart, playing the percentages and being patient for your best scoring opportunities.

The reality is that every green in regulation is a step toward reducing your score. Building on that, if any golfer aims every approach shot at the middle of the green and manages to execute that plan, he or she takes a big step toward making a par. Two-putting from 25 to 30 feet for par all day is hardly ever going to ruin a scorecard.

If you do miss the green—hopefully not on the short-side if you made a prudent Price-esque shot selection—the task now is to scramble and save par. Now you don't have to be heroic like Seve. Instead, select the simplest, highest-percentage shot possible. The easiest one from off the green—certainly the least disastrous shot—is often a putt from off the green. The next most simple shot is the chip (or bump-and-run). Nick shared with me how to hit it: *"The bump-and-run with a 7-iron was one of my favorite shots. I always tried to put the ball a little bit farther back in my stance, hood [close] the club a little bit, take a little bit of loft off with my hands in front, and then take it to the inside, on the on the way back, and try and hook them a little bit. When you hook a chip shot, it doesn't spin [backward] as much. So it's less prone to getting caught up in some longer grass or some adverse conditions, whether there's a divot, or a bit of sand, or whatever. The more spin that you put on a chip, the more it's going to sort of stutter through those areas that aren't so smooth."*

This is all-time advice from an all-time golfer. Sadly, many of today's young golfers seem averse to using a lower-lofted club around the greens. Instead, they want to use the much lower-percentage approach: the unnecessary lob shot. If you are one of those golfers, imagine Nick Price alongside a green with you, and he's telling you how to hit the shot. I imagine you'd listen and at least try it. You'll likely find how easy the shot is. Practicing low shots like this is a sure-fire way to improve touch and feel for better distance control on chip shots. Further it will teach you to understand how different grasses—in different conditions—react to various styles of bump-and-runs. As Nick mentioned, the shot just takes a little practice to learn how much the ball flies, runs, and releases.

Nick then pivoted to the topic of when to add loft to green-side shots, and you'll hear Ballesteros's influence. Seve—the master-craftsman and shot-maker—was a wizard with a wedge and he learned how to create different shots with his 56-degree sand wedge. Nick elaborated, *"If you can take your three or four wedges, and you can hit three different types of shots with each one of them, be it a lob [shot], or a little hook shot. Or just a regular shot that you would play the regular amount of loft. That now gives you three different options with four clubs. That's 12 different options when you get to the green to play. If you've got those 12 different shots, it's very hard to get you behind the 8-ball."*

Nick Price: friendly, curious, patient, hard-working, and ever-learning. The Zimbabwean was gifted with the ability to strike a golf ball, but by way of an open mind, an impressive work ethic, and the desire to learn and experiment, he turned himself into a prolific tournament winner. He's one of my favorites, and writing this chapter has inspired me to call him and learn more from him.

I just felt like my mind and my swing had become a pretzel, and I had to like unravel it and then re-ravel it back together. So it just felt like it was just going to take some time.

Max Homa

7

Max Homa

THE BEAUTY OF THE STRUGGLE

Thoughtful, candid, authentic, and funny, Max Homa shot to prominence and became a fan favorite on social media when he took to roasting people's golf swings. He's a bright light on the PGA Tour, simply a great competitor.

In my opinion, Max has one of the prettiest and most fundamentally sound swings in the game. Whenever I'm dispatched to cover him or his group, I find myself wondering if his golf swing fell out of heaven.

Max has twice been a guest on my *On the Mark* podcast. Once a few years into his pro career after being a national champion at the University of California-Berkeley in 2016, and again in 2020 during the Covid-19 pandemic.

I remember Max being light-hearted and easy-going in the first appearance. The most memorable observation—or certainly the one that lodged in my memory—was when Max shared how he would watch and learn from great PGA Tour players.

Early in his professional career, Homa vacillated

between the PGA Tour and the Korn Ferry Tour, but he eventually established himself as a mainstay on the PGA Tour with a victory in 2019 at Quail Hollow. He's never looked back since.

When we chatted in 2020, Max was still Max, but there was now a palpable maturity about him. He was still authentic and light-hearted, but he spoke with an intellectual humility and a measured confidence; in my opinion, his is a manner born of the ups and downs he navigated during those formative years of being on and off the Tour. He certainly doesn't take success for granted.

I asked him about if there were any lessons learned during those challenging years. He answered by explaining a lesson he shared, from his experiences, with a young member of the Cal golf team. Max told him, *"Figure out what the best part of your game is and then set up a plan to work your game around that. But that's who you are. For me, I'm a good iron player. So when I'm struggling with other parts of my game, I'm going to set up the rounds to showcase my iron play. And also in the meantime, I'm not going to focus too hard on working on it at home, if I need to work on other things. So I think you need to have an identity in the game of golf. I think that's the difficult thing to do. But after that, you just set up a plan and you stick to it for as long as you can, and if you realize along the way that maybe your plan's not right you, adjust."* It's apparent that Max must have kept a pretty level head through his slump in form. This is the first thing I would stress to a golfer in distress: don't panic! Keep your wits about you even though it seems like it's impossible to play well. The truth is everything is fixable if you remain patient and pragmatic. All too often, struggling golfers fall prey to emotion, which will lead them to make irrational decisions, and further mayhem and disappointment ensues.

In Max's case, when he was trying to find his form in

his mid-20s, he knew that his mental game was sound, and he just needed to tighten up his swing mechanics. His plan involved a swing change: *"I was fortunate enough that my plan was my golf swing, and my mental approach to it ended up being right. But I thought that sticking to it was always the hardest part, because there's a lot of uncertainty whether or not you're on the right path."* The truth is there's always an element of risk in changing to turn your form in a positive direction, but sometimes you just have to do it. It goes without saying that if you don't, there's every likelihood that you'll continue along in your own golfing mire.

Once you make a reasonable change, you must commit to the change. The worst thing is to be wishy-washy and half-hearted about what you're doing. Max explains, *"so you got to take a chance here and there and just trust that you're gonna make the right decision. And if you don't, you don't, but at least you stuck to something, and you gave it your all. That's kind of all you can really ask for, especially in sports."* No change will take root unless you have complete commitment and confidence in it.

Max is human, so he did struggle with a thing or two. He shared another of his perspectives, which—thanks to hindsight—embodies a mental and emotional fortitude that is rare among even the elite. Max says, *"I will say that the beauty of the struggle I had, for sure, is that I do try and take time here and there, and think about how cool it is, where I am now. Because I think, for a while, if you would have told me I was going to be 71st-ranked player in the world, I would have kind of scoffed a little bit. Although I believed it, it did seem so far away. So I try and appreciate it, and I try to remember that because it does keep you light and positive and appreciative of this kind of life."* What a wonderful way of looking at things given that in his 2017 season he was unsure if he was going to continue playing professionally. While a pro golfer should never stop aspiring to improve, it's helpful to appreciate where you are and what you've accomplished. Gratitude may not be a huge motivator, but countless golfers lack such a perspective, to the detriment of their games.

Regardless of where you are in life or in your golf game, it's important to stay positive and keep going. Max remembers, *"In 2017, for a little while there, I wasn't sure how much longer I could do this for. It's a fond memory that I try and remind myself of ... just to keep me from being ever negative about any bad round I play."* Ask yourself, how often do you remind yourself of the good things that have happened on the golf course? Most golfers don't do that. In fact, they tend to do the opposite and only remember the bad shots and the putts missed. Our memories can shape our view of ourselves, so be careful how you choose to frame your past to yourself.

On an even deeper level, have you ever looked back on a bad experience and remembered it fondly? Max did, and I believe that it's one of the cornerstones to his success, because he is able to maintain perspective and gratitude in all situations. I'm a firm believer that everything works for good, if you choose to look for the good in everything. It's a trait that I see in the great Gary Player. That man is incredibly positive and has developed the habit of finding the best in every situation.

If nothing else, always remember that the hard times are making you stronger. They are teaching you patience and perseverance, and perseverance leads to maturity and wisdom. So, be thankful for tests and trials and learn to look at them as a part of your growth toward being your best self and certainly the best golfer you can be.

Max Homa is a product of his environment. He spent his childhood in Valencia, near Los Angeles and like Freddie Couples, Max grew up on a public golf course. He explains that he was *"super lucky again. We had a great junior program at our public golf course: it's a par-61 golf course called Vista Valencia. So no par fives, a lot of par threes, and we also had a nine-hole par-three course called Chica. We had a bunch of great players come through there."* Don't you just love Max's attitude? Here's a guy who grew up on a distance-challenged public course and believes he was "super lucky" to do so. Attitude is everything. And I'm convinced that Homa's attitude helped him through the tough times early in his professional career. After all, if literally nothing you do is good enough for you, or enjoyable for you, or remarkable to you, how long do you think you'll continue trying? I'm sure a young Max would be amazed to learn that his older self would get even half as far as he has.

He continued, *"No, we would play there obviously all the time. Play the par-three course mostly, honestly, it wasn't super demanding, but you sure learned how to make birdies. You know, even as a kid I thought that was always important. And I thought that also just made it more fun. I think that a full 18 holes at times could be four to five hours, and it's hard to hold the kids' attention span for that long. But when it's a nine-hole, par-three course, you can run through it. We would play it time after time, and I thought that it grew our love for the game, and also sharpened our skills as we went around."* This anecdote reminded me of something I used to do when I was a college coach. Every so often, just to throw the team a curveball and keep them on their toes, I would have my men's team play off the forward tees. A few positive things usually occurred when we did this. First, they would shoot lower scores, and as a result team morale would typically improve. Second, as Max pointed out, the mindset of making birdies and shooting lower scores would help the guys to reframe their attitudes, especially in the winter when scoring was difficult. Third, with the men having to hit more wedge shots into targets, their scoring elements and wedge skills would trend upward. As a result, on regular-length courses, their birdie production would increase.

Try it! Whatever tees you play from, move a few tees forward and play from there. Alternatively, you can just play from the 200-, 150-, or 100-yard markers. Play nine holes and see how low you can shoot. For advanced players, I make the 150- or 100-yard examination a par 27, and the 200 or beyond a par 36. It may help your perspective and hone other parts of your game.

You have read in previous chapters about the value of playing with golfers of more advanced skill levels. Max spoke of this when he reminisced about his time in college. *"Yeah, I couldn't agree more about the value of competition. When you're practicing, I don't think that there's a set way to do it. I think you hear a lot of people talk about whether you should practice in blocks, or if you just vary your practice. I think that there's no right way to do it. But I feel like if you can sprinkle in some competition with players, either your level or better, it'll make you grow as a player."* For what it's worth, I advocate that all golfers, not just tournament players, plan practice sessions that encompass:

- Block practice (working with one or two clubs with a focus on drills and technique improvements),

- Variable or skills practice (working and focusing on skill acquisition and development on elements such as trajectory variation and contact off uneven and adverse lies), and

- Competition (both on the course and off, with both a full or limited set of clubs).

Max elaborated on the Cal team practices: *"We were very lucky in college to have such a great team and so many great players come through. We would do chipping and putting contests nearly every day of practice."* Cal had an incredible team with a number of players who would make it to the PGA Tour. Max referenced his college teammates: *"Brandon Hagy and Michael Kim and Ben An and Michael Weaver and Pace Johnson and Joel Salter—all these great, great players. And we would just play against each other in any game you could imagine all the time, and I thought we all got better because of it."* You've heard the phrase, a rising tide lifts all boats. Well, it's also true of competitive practice.

Max did get better enough to win the NCAA individual title, and then he turned professional. In 2013 he was offered a few exemptions into PGA Tour events, and in his first start he finished top 10 at the Frys.com Open: an event he would later win ... twice. He followed that up with a top 30 in the following event in Las Vegas.

Max was flying high. He shared the story of how his agent told him to manage his emotions and expectations: *"My agent said, 'Hey, I'm really proud of you. That was great, but I don't want you to think it's this easy; you're probably gonna hit a bump in the road,' and I told them I knew."* Sadly, Max hit that inevitable bump, and he struggled with his game and confidence for a few years. The lesson here is that this awesome, yet wretched game we love so much can take us from the highest of highs to the lowest of lows. All the while, we have to maintain a calm-and-collected manner, and have a complete and honest assessment of our skills, tendencies, strengths, and weaknesses, as we strive to keep focus on what we need to do to bring out our best as often as possible. Despite struggling for a few seasons, Max never stopped working hard and grinding out good results. It's how you react and respond. I find that all great champions have a stick-to-it-iveness that keeps them coming back despite being bruised mentally and physically. Shake it off.

Homa kept a clear head through it all and eventually decided to split with his coach and to go back to his former coach, Les Johnson. There's a valuable lesson in his recount of the story: *"The best way I can say it is I just felt like my mind and my swing had become a pretzel, and I had to like unravel it and then re-ravel it back together. So it just felt like it was just going to take some time. My coach before that ... It was all good stuff, but I just don't think that my brain was connected to it the way it needed to. And I think that's the most interesting thing about player-coach relationships. You know, you got the smartest coach in the world, but if your brain isn't hearing it the right way, or your ears aren't hearing it the right way, there's no there's no way of combating that."* I hope that every aspirant golfer hears that lesson. The student-teacher or player-coach relationship is so very important, and it's defined by the quality of their communication. (In Chapter 17, David Leadbetter will say communication is the most important thing in teaching.) I have long maintained that my message is only as good as what it is understood. Find someone you work well with, who understands you and your swing, who knows how to communicate effectively with you, and who you understand to the point where it brings results.

Of course, that's easier said than done. Sometimes it takes courage to try out another voice, another perspective. And often it takes time to honestly assess if your direction or coach is working. Max all but summarized my beliefs in this area as he continued: *"Like I said before, you could have the most knowledge of anybody in the game. But that doesn't mean it's going to work for everybody. It's no knock on any coach. My coach, Les, probably wouldn't work [well] for some other people. But we think so similarly that it's easy. We can kind of finish each other's thoughts as far as the golf swing goes, but I just think in general golf, there's just no right way to do it."* Homa's perspective here can help you to take a managerial stance in the development of your game, and you should understand where you and your coach are going and how you are planning to get there. Over-communicate rather than under-communicate, ask good questions, and take ownership of your game.

Max eventually made his way back onto the PGA Tour, and he got his first win at Quail Hollow in 2019. I asked him to revisit that experience of winning, and in so doing he shared lessons on dealing with intimidation, playing your own game, dealing with nerves, keeping a good attitude, finding the positive in every situation, good course management, and hitting a good shot at an important time. He started with a recount of the third round alongside Rory McIlroy: *"Well I played with Rory on Saturday, and I thought that was a blessing, as kind of intimidating as it was. But I held my own. I played okay. I ended up getting into the final group. Playing that last day, I felt less nerves than playing with Rory. Just because of Rory, you know, he's an intimidating guy with his game, and the way he hits his driver and all that. That was my first time playing with him."* See? Even the pros get nervous and intimidated. What you feel, they feel too. They just manage themselves and their routines to mitigate the effects a little bit.

Nerves aren't all bad, and it's important to think about them in a positive way. Max relates, *"I think when you're confident in where your game's at, which is how I felt, even if you are nervous, it's good nerves. You still have that swagger and that good positive attitude about the shots that you can hit and the putts that you can make."* To be honest, I was somewhat surprised when Max, who had struggled for a few years, looked almost bullet-proof over the final nine holes of the tournament. I asked about that. Max joked that he *"putted out of his mind for the entire week"* but he did elaborate on the nerves he felt: *"No yeah, I was nervous. I just felt the confidence that I'm a great golfer again. I think that a lot of people are different. I think some people can convince themselves that they are a great golfer without having a result or something tangible. I've always had a hard time doing that. I wish I could just tell myself you [are] really good without any significant evidence, but like I said, when you're playing well and you go play with Rory McIlroy, in the second-to-last group on the weekend at a PGA Tour event and you're holding your own, I think that for me, that was my tangible evidence that I'm pretty good at this."*

Everybody gets nerves. It's a biologically natural response, so don't let anybody tell you not to feel nervous. Trying to avoid nerves just exacerbates the problem, because then you'll start to think about the nerves, think that it's some sign that you don't have what it takes, and then you'll get concerned and anxious when you can't control the nerves or your negative thoughts. Instead, extract something positive from any and every situation. Doing so will help you to channel the nervous energy for good. To this day, I tell my daughters—Isabel who plays golf and Sophia who plays tennis—that the feeling they are feeling prior to a competition or something important, is their "super juice' that's flowing through their bodies. That super juice makes them a super version of themselves. When you feel nerves, embrace the feelings, imagine you have a cape on your back, and go ahead and move forward with confidence and the conviction that you're activated and ready to be a superhero.

As you well know, confidence is mercurial: it comes and goes in the blink of an eye. I'm firmly of the belief that everybody is just one good swing or shot away from a change in momentum. Similarly, the opposite is sadly also true, but what everyone needs to do is keep an open mind to the good, and not just the bad. For example, many of us remember times when we were unlucky in golf, but it's hard for us to remember times we were actually lucky. I learned from Gary Player that I must look for good breaks and, even more, I must expect them. Then when the good fortune occurs, I must recognize it and bank it in my memory. That realization is often the key that unlocks a positive change in form. In some ways, Max identified that too: *"I felt like I was more confident because I started to really realize I was pretty good at this. You need to believe. You need to be your biggest fan, and I think after that Saturday [at Quail Hollow] I started to believe it, and then obviously after Sunday, I believed that even a little bit more."*

I was hanging on Max's every word as he walked me, and the listeners, through the last three holes at Quail Hollow. Those three holes—known as the Green Mile—are beasts, riddled with disaster. The 17th might be one of the hardest par threes I have ever seen: it's 200+ yards, downhill, to an undulating, firm green with water short and left of the target. It has claimed its fair share of misery in professional and non-professional events. I asked Max about how he got by the 17th unscathed, while under the highest of pressure. He responded with a mindset, one that is advisable to any golfer of any skill level: *"I think the most important thing ... one of my best buddies, he's always say 'aggressive swings to conservative targets.'"* I want to stop there and point out that in all of the on-course playing lessons I have given, I notice amateur golfers do the opposite of Max's advice. Most amateurs make defensive, hesitant, uncommitted swings to overly aggressive targets. How can a tentative swing produce the heroic result being asked of that situation? Max continued, *"So when you pick your line on 17, you're almost never going to aim right at the pin, just because of the dangers of being just a little left. So my caddie and I picked the line—a little to the right side of the green, right edge of the green—and I just tried to make a very aggressive swing to that spot. Instead of making a golf swing that's saying, 'don't go left' or 'don't go right.'"* He wasn't aiming at the flag, which would've been ill-advised—but he made an aggressive swing to his safer target. Don't be tentative.

Max continued: *"I'm going to still try to hit the best shot I can hit. That's always my advice to amateurs or people trying to grow with the game. You still have to trust that you can make your golf swing. I don't think we ever hit a ball on the range where we think,* okay, don't hit it left on this one. *We just hit the ball. Again, you have to be your biggest fan and you have to say to yourself, I'm gonna pull the shot off. And that doesn't mean I need to aim straight at the pin or cut it off the water. I'm just gonna make a good swing, and the ball is gonna react appropriately."* Now you might be saying, that sounds all fine and dandy, but it's not as easy for me than for the pros. Well, that's where practice, rehearsal, and developing a go-to shot comes in. Remember Butch Harmon's pearl that he shared: practice for tough situations, and have a go-to shot that you can hit under pressure. (Collin Morikawa will talk about the importance of creating a go-to shot as well, in Chapter 9.)

Max did elaborate on how he hit a quality shot on the 17th: *"I just I got really, really focused on what I was trying to do—the visualization of it, the shot shape—and fortunately I again just trusted that if I get up there and do my stuff, the ball's gonna listen."* This quote is a prime example of what sports psychologists and pro golfers are talking about when they talk about sticking the process. The process is all of the things that take place before the shot is hit. All of those disciplined, mental, and emotional processes that put the athlete in the place to trust and react athletically during the swing. And to Max's point, rest assured that if you do what you should, the ball will listen and oblige. It doesn't have a brain, and despite our suspicions, it only does what our clubface tells it to do.

So when you are faced with that daunting, difficult shot, take your time, dial in, and plan for the shot. Make a positive, directed rehearsal swing. Aim appropriately and commit to that target. Let you last look and your last thought be one of the ball traveling to your target. As Dr. Bob Rotella said, *"I don't know how, but the golf ball knows what you're thinking. Most Tour players will say that the ball usually goes where their last thought is, so if I can get my head in the right place, I will be in pretty good shape."* Focus on what you have control over. Focus on the positive. Once you have that image and that visual, step in and swing freely into a balanced finish. Then go on and go through the exact process on the next shot. After all, every shot, no matter how scary, or easy it is, is only worth one stroke on the scorecard.

I always look forward to my chats with Max Homa. He's easy with a smile and more intellectual than most people think, and I love his insights on competitive golf. He may be casual and affable on social media, but when he's inside the ropes, he's focused, determined, positive, and all business. But when he's off the course, he has a sharp sense of humor and a delightful, self-effacing wit. He is a laugh a minute. Max made me crack up when he said, *"I got multitude of issues. I can't seem to figure it out. But what I usually like to point out with my golf swing is all the arm hair, and it's just distracting. So sometimes when I make a bad swing, hopefully people are more focused on the issues I've got in the hair department rather than the actual swing."* As a middle-aged man, I can think of some much worse hair problems to have.

Teach 'em that basically the ball reacts to the clubface relative to the path, and where the face is relative to the path determines the curvature. And so we have to arrange our body in a manner that allows the club to attack the golf ball on a correct path—and face relative to that—to hit in on line. Drawers swing differently to faders; faders swing differently to drawers; high-ball hitters, low-ball hitters … they're all different.

Mike Adams

8

Mike Adams

Owning Your Unique Swing

As one of the foremost minds in American golf instruction, Mike Adams is a man who needs little introduction. He's a member of the World Golf Teachers Hall of the Fame and a PGA National Teacher of the Year ... and those are just two of his many accolades. Based in northern New Jersey, he's also a top-five ranked teacher according to *Golf Digest*. Such is his stature in my mind that when Terry Rowles set Mike Adams up for an *On the Mark* interview, I was beyond excited.

I will never forget the video chat. Mike was in his car, straight off the lesson tee: a place where he has spent the bulk of his work life. He is casual, yet engaged; soft-spoken, yet full of authority and gravitas. Adams is a man of few words: thoughtful and measured. His delivery of axioms, theories, and assessments drip with a concern for the receiver of the information, and he always works hard to make sure the whoever's listening understands.

Given my respect for him, I felt a twinge of nerves any time I made any sort of remark about golf instruction during our talk. In my mind, I felt like he must've been quietly grading me. The truth was that my worries couldn't have been further from the truth. Mike is like a friendly teddy bear, except this teddy bear has forgotten more about golf instruction than most people will ever learn.

The thrust of our conversation—and pretty much the North Star to his teaching philosophy—pertained to the fact that every golfer has their own swing, which is based on that player's personal physical constitution, and that this fact should be supported by their teaching pro.

As I mentioned, Mike is a stickler for communication and understanding, and more than once he uttered that before the work begins, *"The student needs to understand what the goal is."* This understanding is crucial to any long-term success. All too often, I encounter students who show up for a lesson with no tangible concept of what they are trying to achieve. They know they aren't playing well, and they're looking to improve, but their approach is not granular enough. Worthwhile, successful lessons occur when the student is acutely aware of the issue, has and provides real-time anecdotes from the course, and shares plenty of information with the teacher. If they don't come prepared and equipped, then there's every likelihood that the teacher will just touch on the most glaring issue.

Truth be told, the teacher should also ask the learner to open up the lines of communication and establish the goals, but the onus lies on the lesson-taker. You wouldn't set out on a six-day hike without a plan, would you? Most certainly not! And let me tell you that no player on the PGA Tour embarks on any sort of change until it has been thoroughly vetted, with its path and goals defined.

So, successful students have goals. If you don't have a goal, have your teaching pro explain what they believe is the best goal for you, as well as the path to achieve that goal, so that you have something by which to gauge development and improvement.

Mike also has a wonderful way to talking about the overall action of the body while emphasizing the golf club. He is also a master at sticking with priorities, and he rarely progresses before the task at hand is satisfied. Consider this simple, yet fervent observation: *"we teach 'em how to hit the ball square. We want to get the club-face square on the middle of the golf ball. And once we get that happening, we start to up the speed by getting them to utilize the ground better."* If every golfer abides by Adams' simple advice, there would be many fewer golfers struggling with the game.

With the advent of 24/7 golf media, and access to golf advice at the click of a link, an aspirant golfer can find ideas and opinions in the blink of an eye. While there are certain benefits to this access, there is also a downside: I know I can sound like a broken record here, but misinformation and misunderstanding are rampant. We all want to play better golf, and so while scrolling through social media, lots of swing tips seem appealing, and we begin to wonder if we should try this or try that. But this is like a wolf in sheep's clothing. You wouldn't change your approach to dental care because of some video on social media; instead, you'd still follow the recommendations of your dentist. Though golf instructors are not PhDs or MDs, these swing doctors have studied everything so you don't have to. And the better ones are true teachers: ones who can cater their expertise to you and your particular ways of learning.

We all know this, but remind yourself when watching swing videos that not every swing tip out there will universally benefit everyone. Mike says, *"Drawers [of the ball] swing differently to faders; faders swing differently to drawers; high-ball hitters, low ball hitters they're all different."*

Which leads us to Adams' first piece of advice: Know thyself, and don't take another person's medicine.

This fact can often go overlooked too, amid all the complicated fads in online instruction. Mike reminds us that the face of your golf club is the only way you get to message the golf ball. It's the only direct influence; everything else is an indirect influence.

Now we have Adams' second piece of advice: The golf ball listens to your clubface, and to the clubface alone. Mike Adams constantly preaches about the importance of the clubface, and as a result, he gravitates toward a student's grip on the club, which is how we best control that clubface.

I'd recommend these two axioms to every golfer of every skill level. Like fashion, golf instruction tends to be strongly influenced by its own fads and trends; I could opine on this forever, but I guess that's for another book. As a result, I find innumerable golfers trying tips to improve their power off the tee while being unable to hit the ball solidly, consistently.

Trust me: elite PGA Tour players—check that, every tour golfer—hits the ball solidly nearly every time. The shot may not necessarily be on target, but the contact would be clean and solid. This is a key to good golf, and any player of repute will tell you so. It sounds obvious, but a ball struck in the sweet spot of the clubface is not only more powerful, it's more aerodynamic and efficient, so it performs significantly better in the wind. A well-struck ball makes club selection easier, and to me—most importantly—solid contact mitigates the subconscious tendency to over-swing and over-hit a shot. This strategy creates a great feedback loop, in which a well-timed, well-sequenced swing leads to better ballstriking, and better ball-striking allows a well-timed and sequenced swing. Finally, in terms of the playability and proximity of an approach shot, a well-struck shot lands pin-high more often than not. (We'll discuss this more in Chapter 12, when Hal Sutton shares the advice he got from Raymond Floyd: hit the ball pin-high every time.)

Following on from the focus on well-struck shots, and remaining true to Mike Adams' teaching priorities, the addition of power should be measured and governed. While the use of ground-reaction force generates speed, the golfer must understand how this speed is actually transmitted to the golf club and eventually the golf ball.

Adams contends that a golfer's legs will respond to the arms: *"A simple way to increase speed is to allow the arms to swing faster. Get your grip right, and swing the arms faster ... then the legs immediately begin to move faster."* Faster arms do indeed lead to a faster body, but everything has to be under control and stay in sync. He also made this point, worthy of extra attention: *"Only when the golfer has control of the club handle and the clubface will he be able to [properly] amplify the swing speed using the legs and torso. If the legs and torso were first focused on, it is highly likely that the clubface will be inconsistenly presented through impact, and contact and control—and hence shot quality—will be compromised."* I'd love you to re-read this nugget, meditate on it, and allow it to settle in your psyche. Consistency is king.

Mike and I have both seen too many golfers "popping" all over the place, in an attempt to use the ground and create speed. In the end, this folly ends in poorly struck, inconsistent, and crooked golf shots. Adams calls the malady *"swinging with powerless effort instead of effortless power."* It reminds me of a saying I got from my club pro when I was about 14 years old: "The rough is littered with golfers who tried to hit the ball too hard."

So remember, grip the club appropriately, understand your grip's influence on the clubface and how you need to move in support of it to hit the ball squarely in the face. When you have that resolved, use this simple and highly effective drill Mike Adams shared: *"What we've found is a simple way—if you stand there and you swing continuously five times, continuous back and forth, back and forth, back and forth, [your] feet will arrange themselves in a position that allows them to create force and balance. It's amazing ... let them discover it."* What a wonderful way to find your place to connect with the ground and understand foot flare: the way your feet are splayed and angled to best facilitate your fastest, most efficient way of swinging. After all, how can you employ and exploit ground-reaction force if you aren't properly set up? That would be like the 100-meter sprinter trying to win the race after being improperly set up in the starting blocks.

Every good swing is born out of the ground and in your hands. Mike Adams knows that, and he never deviates from that important maxim. He's is a teacher's teacher who has spurned a cadre of fantastic golf instructors, a man who is most comfortable on the driving range, with a student or an aspirant instructor. I can still hear him reciting, *"a good teacher has a method, a great teacher has several methods, [and] a super star teacher [has] a system that includes all methods and [only] utilizes the ones that apply to the student."* So if you want to seek instruction, be sure to have a goal, work on a plan to achieve that goal, and find an teacher-instructor who'll respect your unique swing. And work on that clubface!

I think people learn the best when you teach yourself: when you are the one who will actually be telling the words, and interpreting yourself, because that's the best way. You know how to tell yourself a certain way; everyone has different feels.

Collin Morikawa

9

Collin Morikawa

You Can't Skip a Step

Collin Morikawa is a bona-fide star. Charismatic, intelligent, well-spoken, and of course talented, Collin burst out of the NCAA ranks onto the PGA Tour. After an All-American career at the University of California-Berkeley, Morikawa turned pro in summer 2019. It took the Californian just six events to earn his first tour victory. Then it was off to the races for arguably the preeminent iron-striker of his generation. Morikawa has quickly amassed five victories, including two majors: the 2020 PGA Championship and the 2021 Open Championship. His résumé is already glittering, and he's most certainly one of the leading players in the game.

Collin joined me for a chat on the *On the Mark* podcast while the PGA Tour was paused during Covid-19 in spring 2020. Our conversation was easy and tremendously informational, with Collin sharing thoughts from his favorite club to his mental game and course strategy. He impressed me mightily, and I believed the charming young man was on the fast track to the top. Little did I know that he would win his first major just four short months after our chat.

The first thing that struck me about Morikawa was how savvy, organized, and singular he was in his pursuits. Golf pundits call it your golf IQ; in life, people refer to it as being wiser than your years, or having an old head on young shoulders. Collin knows where he and his game are going, and his manner is a great model for any aspirant golfer. He shared his thoughts from when he was just 18 years old, arriving at Berkeley: *"When I took that first step into my freshman year, I knew what steps I had to take to kind of get to the PGA Tour. I already had my game analyzed. I knew what kind of player I was. So I had to really sit down and take those four years and realize, you know, I had to work on my short game. It was the number one thing—everything from wedges, to bunker play, to chipping to putting, you know: everything inside 100 yards. I had to work on."*

Two main observations jump out at me from Morikawa's remark. First, nothing happens by accident with great athletes and players. Collin was prepared and he had researched what he had to do to maximize his time in college. He understood his strengths and weaknesses, thanks to data capture and analysis, and he resolved to beef up his weakness. I'm reminded of my friend Nick Price (Chapter 6): a similar expert with iron play, who realized that the short game was the deficiency that he needed to improve in order to compete at an elite level.

Second, every golfer can improve their short game. In an era when power is sexy, too many golfers think they can improve performance by simply becoming a great ball-striker. The truth is that this approach will only get you to a certain point. Week-in and week-out on tour, the best ball-striker who scrambles and putts the best typically wins. Again, this was Price's observation in the '90s as well. And more importantly for amateurs, the golfer who can recover from peril is the golfer who usually is the most consistent scorer. My hero Bobby Jones once said, "The secret to golf is to turn three shots into two." It's possible to do that around every green. I often say, if a golfer gets better at his third shot on every hole, he's going to make lots of 3s and 4s. To put another way: improving your tee shot will lead to fewer big numbers. Improving your third shot will lead to more small numbers. If you get that third shot—be it an approach on a par five, or a chip or long putt on a par 4—close to the hole to make a four, you'll make a lot of birdies and pars. Who doesn't need more of those on their scorecard? Eighteen 4s add up to 72.

On the subject of development and improvement, Morikawa's longtime coach Rick Sessinghaus impressed upon Collin the ideas of self-discovery and ownership of one's game. Rick has been a guest on the *On the Mark* podcast a few times, and it's his belief that if a golfer takes complete ownership of their game, then the results—especially under pressure—are all but guaranteed to improve. Rick shared with me that he would teach a young Morikawa a concept, and then he would leave Collin to his own devices for a while, enabling a period of self-discovery when Collin could tinker with the lesson and own it all. Collin referenced this method in our discussion: *"I think people learn the best when you teach yourself: when you are the one who will actually be telling the words, and interpreting yourself, because that's the best way. You know how to tell yourself a certain way; everyone has different feels."* This quotation sounds very similar to some of Fred Couples' comments in Chapter 2, and you'll hear it in how Nick Faldo translated his work with David Leadbetter in Chapter 17. It's a regular breakthrough for the best players.

Collin is so correct with this assessment. The big challenge as a learner is to take a cerebral concept and make it a "feel." And naturally, all golfers have their own feels. These periods of self-discovery—when a player is free to roam anywhere within the parameters of the lesson or advice—are golden. After this time of getting comfortable with a lesson, making it a feel, the key is then cemented for future reference. I asked Collin if he commits things to memory or if he writes things down. Given his professional demeanor, his response was what I expected: *"I do write things down, especially when it comes to the short game."* When Collin was a student, he studied golf and his golf swing. It's clear that this rigorous style of study has continued into his professional career.

There's a seriousness, involving an intentional discipline of study and note-taking, that many great players have about game improvement. They know where they are going, and they can chart where they've been. Just like the explorers centuries ago, when on voyages of discovery, you should be diligent and meticulous enough to chart your course and keep notes along the journey. This journey through golf has—and will have—many twists and turns, and successful people rarely make the same mistake twice. You also don't want to get lost along the way.

Morikawa addressed the importance of notes, and how they help him get back to where he was when he needs to: *"I think when things get out of sorts, it's not necessarily I've got to change anything, I've just got to go back to my basics. And those are things that I write down. I go back to the basics of checking alignment, checking my weight, checking where my arms are; those are the biggest things because I think a lot of people day to day, you know, their bodies feel different. Everything's different and you want to feel the same when you set up to the ball."* If even tour pros—who do this full time and have the most consistent, repeatable swings on the planet— keep notes to review their basics and check their positions, you should too.

On your long journey of game improvement, it's worthwhile to have a goal, or an idea of where you want to end up, and a plan on how to get there. While I recommend dreaming and hoping for long-term, big-reach goals, I recommend setting your smaller, shorter-term goals that are measurable and attainable. Morikawa had this to say about his approach to goals: *"I just set goals for myself. I've told a lot of people that I see expectation different than goals. You know, expectations are what people put on you; goals or what you set for yourself. And I had to kind of look away from everyone's expectations of what me, [Matthew] Wolff, Viktor [Hovland] were going to do this summer, because everyone puts these expectations on us."* That was some sage advice from Morikawa: focus on your personal goals alone ... No one, including the media or public, friends or family, makes your goals for you. It's a lot like Nick Price advising younger players to "be yourself." Hal Sutton shut out the noise of others' expectations, too. You'll read about it in Chapter 12.

A goal should create a positive effect, while expectations often have a negative effect of added pressure. Collin had to constantly renew his mind and focus inward and on his personal goals, rather than letting the external hype, or noise, or criticism affect him. And there was certainly a lot of expectations and hype around his graduating class of college golfers: a banner group of young stars that included Viktor Hovland, Matt Wolff, and Justin Suh.

In my experience—expectations, both internal and external, can truly wreck a golf swing and golf game. Expectations certainly detract from the important focus on progress and improvement, since they are focused only on results. Expectations can cause tension and anxiety that blur the mind and most certainly impede progress. And the harsh truth is that nobody knows what the future holds. Better to focus on what we can work on, what we can control, and not worry about the rest.

And yet, you have to realize that you can't hide from outside expectations, positive or negative—you have to develop a mindset that can acknowledge expectations, but set them aside while you work on your measurable, attainable goals. I believe Morikawa has found a way to manage the pressure of expectations and to remain true to his goals and his plan, despite any circumstance in which he may find himself. I saw this resilience and focus when I asked Collin about playing under pressure in the 2020 3M Open, when he was dueling with his peer, the phenom Matthew Wolff, with whom Collin competed fiercely in college. Here he was, just a few short months after graduating from college, walking down the 72nd hole of a PGA tournament with a chance to win his first professional event. He recalled having the presence of mind to take a little extra time, a few extra breaths, in order to settle his nerves and his mind. Collin says, *"I think I found myself really well to go down that 18th hole; you know, be ready for my tee shot, be ready for my approach shot, and realized I can't be skipping steps of my routine. And I think I might have to take a couple seconds more. For me, I just can't skip steps, because I think when people start rushing—when you get into positions like that—you kind of forget things that you normally might have done, either at the beginning of the round, or in the middle of the day on the Thursday round … so for me, going back to being under pressure like that, simply just for me to open my yardage book, and whether I comprehend that much that I've written down is besides the [point]. It's just for me to have that extra couple of seconds, open the yardage book, you know, have that breath of just seeing what I'm looking at here, and then close it listen up to J. J. [Jacovac—his caddie] to see what we're gonna do."* Hearing Collin acknowledge the pressure of the situation and yet lean on his routine—and slow down, rather than speed up—shows a lot of maturity and poise for a rookie. His thoughts didn't turn to expectations—what people thought or expected of him—and he wasn't wrapped up in the crowd's reactions, which were immense. Instead, Collin went inward: he focused on himself, his routine, and what he needed to do to give the next shot the best chance. Thanks to his preparation, he was just operating in his own little bubble: insular, unhurried, and prepared to do what he's done many times before. He hit the most gorgeous buttercut 5-iron over the top of the flag to about 25 feet. It was a case study in focus, attitude, and execution: a case study that any golfer of any skill level would benefit from.

Let's look back at the goals that got Morikawa to this moment. Speaking of the fade, Collin—like many elite golfers—altered the go-to shape of his golf shots to create more control, and a more easily repeatable swing and result under pressure. Collin explains, *"Coming into college, I was playing a soft draw; let's just say just a little baby draw. And by midway through freshman year, it kind of evened itself out. By the end of freshman year, it started to work to a fade."* The work he was doing with Rick Sessinghaus led him to hitting a fade, but that change happened gradually over time: over an entire season, in fact.

This is a good time to talk about spin. I give this speech to a lot of students: every golf ball spins. The only time it isn't spinning is when it's lying stationary. If a ball is moving, it's spinning. As a result, every swing change manifests a change of spin. Any adjustment should either create more spin or less spin, or it should influence a change in the spin axis of the ball, promoting more right-to-left or left-to-right spin. As far as shot-straightening measures go, very simply put— draw spin straightens a fade shot, and conversely fade spin straightens shots that are drawing too much. So if you want to straighten your slices, don't try and keep your head down: try to hit draws instead. If you want to quell a hook, try to fade the ball in the opposite direction. Remember what Butch Harmon said in Chapter 1: *"I believe in opposites. If you're hitting slices, I'm going to try and make you hit a hook. And you hit hooks, I'm gonna try and make you hit a slice, and you'll meet the middle. You have to understand what they're doing that causes the path to be out-to-in too much in-to-out or whatever it is. But if you go the opposites, it's amazing how they meet in the middle, and it makes things easier."*

Collin talked about continuing his slow swing change and development this go-to cut: *"Once I started my sophomore season, I was hitting 85-90% of fades. And I think that's when my ball striking really changed, because I had a go-to shot. I had that shot no matter where we were—no matter what pin, wind, whatever it was—I had a go-to shot that I could rely on every single time out of the fairway. It's just being able to have that shot for me, you know, the five-, seven-yard cut with any club. I can choke down on a little bit, hit it different heights. But that's the shot. I'm always gonna go to that shot."* The real benefit was that it became Collin's go-to shot that he could rely on when the pressure was high, or when he was a little unsure.

Every golfer should develop and rely on a go-to shot. Even Tiger Woods had a shot he went to under pressure: remember the stinger? Tiger made this highly reliable fairway-finder cool, and every young player tried to adopt this go-to shot, which is also a lot of fun to hit.

Certain players like to work the ball in both directions, but in my opinion—under pressure—that's difficult to execute consistently. And besides, why not try and get consistent with one shot-shape instead of being inconsistent with two shot patterns? Rather than hitting draws 50% of the time, and fades 50%, Collin prefers eliminating one side of the golf course. I can vouch for that. When I'm working on-course for CBS Sports, whenever I'm assigned to

Morikawa's group, I see him hit many small fades. (Unless of course a rare hole or position actually forces him to hit a draw.) The consistent, reliable, controllable baby-fade shot allows him to aim approach shots to right hole locations down the middle of the green. This increases the probability of hitting more greens in regulation. Consider the scenarios: if his fade fades it will be perfect; if it flies straight it will land in the heart of the green; in the worst-case, if he pulls or draws the shot slightly, it can somehow still grab a portion of the putting surface.

Morikawa not only channels his physical gifts, he's also a firm believer in the power of his mind and of the mind-body connection. It's a tactic and routine that elite players have been using for close to 50 years, and Collin continues the tradition: *"When I'm over an iron shot, I think this is what makes me very solid ball-striker, is because I visualize it really well."* Further, he respects the value of each and every shot. A true tactician, like Tiger and Nick Price, Collin doesn't leave anything to chance and will only pull the proverbial trigger when he's mentally and physically in tune. Collin says, *"Visualizing is important. So if I don't feel comfortable over my setup, I'm not going to be able to visualize it. I'm not going to be able to feel and hit that shot. Yeah, so that's when I need to step off, step back, you know, and then re-adjust myself and then step back into the shot."*

This is a lesson for any golfer of any skill level: all parts of your preparation and routine help to inform one another and ensure the best possible result. The technical swing work or practice swing creates a feel, which allows you to reliably visualize the outcome, which gives you confidence in the shot. If one of these things feels off, it's a signal to you to step back and restart the routine. All too often, I see golfers just go ahead and hit a given shot with no conviction whatsoever; they still hit the shot when they are physically uncomfortable over the ball, and their minds are riddled with doubt. Not Collin, or Max Homa, or Hal Sutton, or any elite tour pros. Doubt and indecision are kryptonite to a golf swing or putting stroke, and I would much rather see a golfer hit a wrong shot with conviction than luckily produce the right shot with indecision. I also contend that players make more mistakes before the club is even swung than during the swing. By definition, if some pre-shot element is off-kilter, then some sort of mid-swing compensation or adjustment is necessary. This is a toxic ecosystem that's liable to end with a less-than-desirable result. Collin exudes this notion when he talks about feel: *"Yeah, I'm just all about feel, making sure all my basics and my setups are lined the way I want to hit my shot. And if I think I can feel my swing hitting that shot from that position, there's a green light to go ahead and swing."* In other words, let your routine guide you and free yourself up to hit your best shots.

Let's be honest, Collin Morikawa could be the poster-boy for professionalism, and he has that gorgeous swing to boot. He's always poised and in control. It's enviable, and it doesn't happen by accident. Like Nick Price did, Collin watches golfers with good short games when he plays practice rounds or even tournament rounds with them. He also watches select players on the range. Learning and borrowing from others is crucial, and everybody should do it. When you are playing with someone who does something very well, watch how they go about their craft. It's like a daily apprenticeship. Copy them, emulate the moves, and not necessarily just their technique; study their routines, and how they practice and prepare. Believe it or not, Morikawa, a multiple major champion steals with his eyes: *"Absolutely, I mean, balance is a huge thing for me... And you know, I like to think for me I still do a lot of balance work. Like I love watching Tiger and Rory [McIlroy] just hit balls on the range. Because especially Tiger now, he's very in control ... he's got to watch what he does. But when he's finishing, he's all the way on that left side. He's standing nice and tall. Rory does the same thing."*

Morikawa is still a very young player, but he exudes experience and well-earned confidence. He's focused on his own goals, not anyone's expectations. He's got an approach to the game that can and will serve him for many years to come. Considering how good he already is, that may be a scary thought for fellow pros.

I find myself coming back to Collin's axiom, "You can't skip steps." Collin has proven that he's developed into an elite player—and major winner—by never rushing a shot or his preparation, or his career.

I'm trying to psychoanalyze myself: stopping, starting, pausing. I try to be a little stoic about things. I'm competitive. I want to beat people, but I don't go out of my way to show you I can beat you. It's more like, I made another putt, or I made four birdies in a row, and I let that speak for itself. And yes, I smile while I'm doing it.

Viktor Hovland

10

Viktor Hovland

I Smile While I'm Doing It

Viktor Hovland is a gem. He's uber-talented, but he doesn't take himself too seriously. He's modest, but forthright. He's funny, but thoughtful. It appears that his soul is always smiling, and most times he can't keep it in: his big smile floods his face and everything around him. I have to admit that whenever I get an on-course assignment with Hovland, I can't help but get excited. Viktor is a heck of a golfer and a dynamite competitor. Proof lies in his 2018 U.S. Amateur victory—where the champion has to win six grueling matches in a row—his impressive stretch of play at the end of the 2023 season, and his already impressive Ryder Cup record. I'll go on the record now and say that if Viktor manages to stay injury-free, he'll win at least one major.

I truly enjoyed hosting Viktor on my *On the Mark* podcast, which was recorded a week or so after the European Team won the Ryder Cup at Marco Simone Golf Club in Rome, Italy. Viktor was back in his hometown of Oslo, Norway. At the top of the conversation, I joked with him that he probably arrived back in Norway to a hero's welcome. Ever effacing, he smiled and responded, *"I wouldn't go that far, but it was really nice to see just kind of normal people walking up to you and saying 'Hey, awesome playing in Italy.' And it seems like a lot of people are starting to watch golf, even though they might not play themselves, and so it's been cool to kind of be a part of getting golf a little bit bigger back home."*

In an era when there is much *talk* about growing the game of golf, Viktor—in his own modest way—is certainly *doing* his part. Such is his allure and his athletic build and playing style that he is garnering more and more interest in golf in Norway: a country where soccer, handball, and winter sports are most popular.

Hovland got his start in golf when his dad brought him a set of clubs from the U.S., but he didn't focus on golf full-time until later in his adolescence. Hovland recalls, *"I also did taekwondo, and I played soccer for a few years, and it wasn't until I was maybe 11 or 12 [that] I decided, hey, that I kind of want to keep playing golf in the winter instead of shutting it down for four or five months."* In my opinion, this is a wonderful insight for all parents of young golfers: if a sport is ever going to stick, it's got to come from the child. The lesson for you with children: golf must be fun, and then they can develop a passion for the game on their own. By all means, have your kids participate in competitions and such, but don't make too big a deal of the results. Winning is fun, but it's not the only thing: otherwise what does that say when you lose, in a sport where everyone loses more often than they win? If a passion is cultivated, it must not be a passion for winning, but rather a passion for the game. If a child feels a passion for the game, then that passion will live with them forever. And it will help them to persevere through the inevitable tough times to come. Secondly, golf is an athletic sport and is becoming more and more so. Golfers at the elite level are fitter, stronger, and faster—they are athletes who play golf. Parents: cultivate the athlete in your child, and when they grow up a little, they will have an advantage over their peers.

One thing about Hovland—and it emanates from him—is that he is single-minded and prepared to make sacrifices when it comes to achieving goals. When he spoke about his decision to go to Oklahoma State, I was struck by this comment: *"We had a great golf course there. Great history in terms of college golf with Oklahoma State, and every person there ... we kind of have the same goals in mind. We wanted to play the PGA Tour, and we want to win a national championship. So for me, just a kid from Norway, it was very easy for me to integrate into that culture."* Let's be honest: it would have been easy for Viktor to go somewhere else, somewhere perhaps a little more like home. In fact, he could have stayed home and turned pro early. Instead, he was attracted by the culture of golf at OSU, and he went beyond his comfort zone to become a part of it so he could set the groundwork for a possible PGA Tour career.

In terms of both personal and game development, Viktor has always had an open mind. I believe that open-mindedness as an attitude, if adopted, is something from which all golfers would benefit. We've heard about its importance already from the great Nick Price. Here's Hovland on his growth mindset: *"I had an open mind to what they have to say. I took a listen to everything they had to say. And if I didn't agree, we just had a really good relationship to where we could discuss things and say, you know, 'Hey Coach, I hear what you're saying, but I don't think that's applicable to me, because I do it this way.' So it's not necessarily you have to just listen to your coach, no matter what he says, but we just created a relationship to where I respect that everything that he had to say, because he wants the best for me. And then we could discuss and talk about it whether that is the best course of action for me."* Viktor has just shared a very important lesson for all golfers that play for coaches or golfers that take lessons from a coach or a teaching professional: you have to know who you are, and you must be brave enough to not just follow a lesson or advice blindly. Be informed and be actively involved with every decision that pertains to your game. Remember that in the end, you are the one with your hands on the rubber end of the club, and thus the buck stops with you. You cannot blame anybody else for your shortcomings. You are the author of your golfing destiny.

Viktor played for Alan Bratton, who before becoming head coach at Oklahoma State was a tremendous player on tours around the world, including the PGA Tour. In other words, Bratton knows what he's talking about when it comes to golf and competition. Yet Viktor had the moxie to sometimes respectfully disagree with Bratton on aspects of game improvement and work.

Viktor was actively involved in the development of his game, but he wasn't myopic. Viktor explains, *"I think just going into it with an open mind, and sometimes if you don't agree just to still listen to the opposite view and see what works for you."* What a wise point of view. You never know where the next secret is going to be uncovered, so be open-minded to information and opinion. Don't be ignorant and just follow without understanding the how and why of it all. Remember, if you have honestly assessed yourself, you have better insight about your strengths and weaknesses than anyone else.

Viktor continued to exhibit his golf IQ as he spoke about his swing and his approach to swing technique: *"Obviously you could find an optimal way to play the game of golf. And we all have our own unique way of doing it. And some things aren't going to work for everyone. So you've got to find your own way to get better. And*

sometimes the path is … not always right in front of you."
See, real improvement does not always happen when you take the path of least resistance. Real, consequential improvement happens when a golfer exhausts every option and works on every department of the game. Viktor continued: *"I think every single player has to kind of look at it like that instead of thinking, 'oh, that's the way he's doing it, so I'm just going to copy him.' And I guess when you take ownership of your own game, it's a lot easier to take that game to the next level."* It's a highly thoughtful and insightful way of looking at swing development. Don't just take the lazy approach of copying somebody else. Instead, take ownership of who you are, and what our game represents, and explore ways to hone that. Be yourself, and swing within yourself.

Hovland used this statement to describe where he feels comfortable, and how his competitive mindset is a little more laid-back, understated, and fun: *"I'm trying to psychoanalyze myself: stopping, starting, pausing. I try to be a little stoic about things. I'm competitive. I want to beat people, but I don't go out of my way to show you I can beat you. It's more like, I made another putt, or I made four birdies in a row, and I let that speak for itself. And yes, I smile while I'm doing it."* It's a good idea for all amateur golfers to just let the results speak for themselves. Act like that great outcome—or for that matter even that bad outcome—is what you expected, that you've done it before, and that you won't be surprised when you do it again.

In this game of golf—where peril is lurking at every turn, and moments will beat you up both mentally and physically—a smile if the best medicine and the best competitive tactic. As Julie Andrews once sung, "a spoonful of sugar helps the medicine go down." I believe a smile helps a golfer's internal temperature go down. Studies have shown that the physical act of smiling—even when you're terribly sad—has a very positive effect on the body. To wax scientific: when you smile, your brain releases chemicals—such as dopamine, serotonin, and endorphins—that lower your anxiety and increase feelings of happiness. You don't even need to do something to smile about: just smile. So for goodness sake, and for your score's sake, smile while you're out on the golf course. A bad day on the golf course is better than a good day in the office.

Owning your swings, shots, and outcomes is important, and you should recognize the good things. I'll never forget Larry Mize, whom I had the good fortune of teaching for about five seasons, say to me: *"if I am going to own my bad shots, then I have to own my good shots too."* In other words, enjoy your good shots. Smile after you smashed that drive. Celebrate after you make that crucial putt. Acknowledge yourself after each small success. Don't just berate yourself after bad shots. You may feel like you aren't being tough enough if you aren't tough on yourself with bad shots. The truth is that feeling despondent or angry will absolutely not help you with your next shot. You're wreaking havoc in your mind, and your body will behave accordingly.

Viktor shared another valuable lesson on course management and the mental game, and it has to do with the relationship to performance and results. He said, *"This is something that I've kind of thought about a little bit recently. It's not looking at the scoreboard that is bad in itself, or not looking. I think it's how you respond to looking at the leaderboard. I think before, I was a little immature, and I didn't have the best short game to get me out of situations. And I saw, okay, wow I'm up on the leaderboard, I'm like two shots behind the lead with nine holes to go. I gotta step up and make some birdies, and then I would short-side myself, make a double bogey, and then I am out of the tournament."* Again, it's not necessarily what happens to you—because bad things will happen to you out there, whether it's a bad shot or bad luck, or both—it's how you react. It's a separator out on tour, that's for sure. Remember that you can't make up three shots with just one swing. Stay patient and play to your strengths. Own your game, trust that good things will happen, and you'll always have a chance.

There's the other side of the coin, too: don't gamble so much on one shot that you give up three strokes with just one swing. Thoughtful and measured in his delivery, Viktor continued: *"A lot of the times if you just play your game, play, like if I have a 7-iron in my hand, and the pin is back-left, I'm just gonna hit it to 20 feet. If I make the putt, great; if I don't, I'm still in the tournament. I'm not going to give the tournament away. If someone goes out there and beats me, that's another thing, but I'm not going to give the tournament away. So I do like to see where I'm at. But I guess right now I'm experienced enough to not let that change my game plan."* Viktor trusts his game and chases the leader steadily. Think of trailing someone in a long running race: you wouldn't try to sprint to get in front of him; instead, keep up with him, keep him in your sights, and if you've got what it takes, you'll overtake him (or he might beat himself!). But don't beat yourself before you get the chance to beat the leader. I'm reminded of Bobby Jones' quote, "The object of golf is to beat someone, make sure that someone is not yourself." Now when a leader sees Hovland's name just behind theirs in a golf tournament, I'm sure it's difficult for them not to worry a bit!

Hovland has worked on technical aspects of his swing, as well as his chipping, but he said there was a more influential change that he made to his game. He explains, *"I've worked hard on my game, and I feel like it's been in a great spot, but I feel like a lot of it was just the mindset kind of change. Instead of trying to be so perfect all the time, I kind of looked at a 72-hole tournament in a different way. Instead of [thinking] 'Okay, I have to shoot 3-under on this side to be in a good spot to have a chance to win the tournament on Sunday,' it was more like 'Okay, my game is good enough. I just have to use the right strategy, trust myself, and I'm gonna get a spurt. We're okay these nine holes, I'm not going to hit it very good, and I just need my short game so get me around make a couple of nice up-and-downs.' Keep myself [thinking], 'Okay, I shot even on this front nine and I know that if I get hot I can really tear this place up.' When things aren't going your way, or you're lipping out putts from 20 feet and you're hitting good shots, but not quite the right distances all the time, I think it's important to tell yourself, 'I'm doing okay. And you know, the next day or the next nine I might play, I might get on a hot streak,' and that's just what I did at East Lake and at Olympia Fields."* Hovland is preaching patience rather than forcing results. After all, when you force something, the better chances are that it won't come off well. Your mind should be helping you play better next hole, next nine, next round, rather than hurting your chances.

As I listened to Viktor, it occurred to me that his anecdotes from his recent wins at the BMW Championship at Olympia Fields and at the Tour Championship at East Lake to win the 2023 FedEx Cup broke down what that word *patience* really means, and I pitched that to him. As you would expect, he giggled as he began his response: *"Yeah, I guess I've just elaborated on the cheesy line 'just trying to stay patient,' but it is so true. It's like, you got to look at a tournament as a 72-hole tournament. And you're not going to win it on the first day, but you can definitely lose it. And I know that my game is good enough, so I don't have to be super nervous the first day I'm teeing it up. I just have to go out there and play my game. Play smart, miss it on the right sides, and I know that if I just take care of my business, I'm gonna have a good chance come Sunday."* Now for amateur golfers reading this, in Viktor's case, he plays 72-hole contests. In contrast, your competitions may be 36 or 18 holes, but the advice remains the same. You're not going to win the event on the first few holes, or on the first day. You can lose it, however, with some rash decision-making and forced swings, so make smart plays and allow the day to unfold. Play into the rhythm of the round. If it starts out hot, great. If you start out a little nervy, don't exacerbate the problem with some overly aggressive plays that—if they don't come off right—serve up bogeys or double bogeys, or worse. You may be surprised by how good an unpressured, calm, and—in some ways defensive—strategy can be for you, both mentally and for your score.

Just like two championship boxers who spar for a little while, feel out the opponent, and wait for the opportune time to unload the haymaker, don't be in a rush to hit your hero shots on the course. As Viktor says, a patient confidence is not only helpful, it's also comforting: *"that thought process is very comforting. I don't have to do anything extraordinary to be up there. I can rely on my short game if my long game isn't on the level that it should be. And it's [like] that more and more often, I can. I'm proving that to myself, that I just become more relaxed in the heat of the moment."* Tension is stress and diminishes your mental and physical facilities; Stay relaxed, poised, and confident, and you'll give yourself the best chance of a good round.

Speaking of being more relaxed in the heat of the moment, Hovland admitted that the most nervous he has ever been on a golf course was at the 2021 Ryder Cup at Whistling Straits. The reason was that he was weak around the greens, and the pressure of the partisan American crowd aggravated the problem. So even stars like Viktor Hovland feel nervous in competition, when the pressure is ramped up. I asked him a bout dealing with the pressure of the 1st tee, specifically the mayhem that was the 1st at Marco Simoné in the 2023 Ryder Cup two years later. I expected his response would likely include a mixture of deep breathing, visualization, and calming techniques. Instead, he spoke of the peace that comes from knowing and owning your golf swing (and a little positive affirmation): *"I think it goes way back to where I feel like I have ownership of my own golf swing. But I think you have to take ownership of what you do. You have to understand your flaws, and how it feels, and if you do a certain thing, what's going to happen. But sometimes you just got to shut that off. And in that moment, you just have to tell yourself, 'Hey, I'm ready. I know I got this.'"*

You can tell that Viktor's all-around game—but more importantly his perspective and confidence—improved a lot in those two years. After all, everything begins in the mind and with beneficial self-talk. *"I think instead of being super nervous in that moment, I kind of embraced that it was more like, 'okay, let's get these crowds riled up and rooting for Team Europe, and I'm just going to pound it down there and put some pressure on the guy.' So that's kind of the mindset, instead of 'Holy crap that fairway looks narrow, I better catch it in the middle of the face.'"* Whether you think you're going to hit a great shot or a poor shot: either way, you're probably right. Let your mind give yourself the best chance for success, and then let yourself play. And don't forget to smile!

Viktor's positive, growth mindset in 2021 greatly helped him become a better player the next year, and the year after that, his growth culminated in a breakout 2023, winning the FedEx Cup and dominating at the Ryder Cup (two of them 4&3, and one 9&7!). He was also in the first or second group in each of the five sessions: the confident pacesetter for the Europeans in the race for the cup. At one point in Rome, Viktor was facing a tough greenside shot and a very difficult decision. His caddie, Shay Knight, advised that perhaps he should putt it to be safe, but Viktor decided to back his newfound greenside improvements and confidence under pressure. Viktor recalls, *"I just thought, 'I'm trying this. I know how to do this. I can hit a low skidding chip-shot into the bank, check it perfectly as it gets over the top and just tickle it down to the hole.'"* Viktor executed exactly what he envisioned: he actually holed the chip and kicked off what was a European Ryder Cup romp. Imagine working so hard on your weakness, that in the highest-pressure situation possible, you choose to face your former weakness and pull it off. That's a true achievement.

I learned a lot from young Viktor during our conversation. He shared so many insights and ways of thinking that will help all golfers find their best. If you haven't already listened, I recommend taking time to do so. Viktor spoke candidly about his short-game deficiencies and how—with logic, stats, and data, and most importantly his open-mindedness—he turned that weakness into a strength. That mentality makes a huge difference, and that's something you must work on and train, as well. And who knows where Viktor will go in the future. But if he sticks to his positive mindset and outlook, I'm sure he'll be a force in the game for many years to come.

Often the real truth is surprisingly simple.

Karl Morris

11

Karl Morris

DECIDE THE GOLFER THAT YOU'RE GOING TO BE

Karl Morris is a name you may not have heard of, but in my opinion, he is one of the great minds in golf instruction. In fact, I enjoy his company so much that I have featured him three times on my *On the Mark* podcast.

Widely regarded as Europe's leading golf performance coach, Morris has a stable of current and former clients that reads like a "Who's Who" of European golf. Lee Westwood, Louis Oosthuizen, Darren Clarke, Graeme McDowell, Paul McGinley, and Ian Woosnam have all sought out his logical, insightful counsel. Karl is the brains behind The Mind Factor: Karl's approach to practical coaching, largely based on his experiences as a former European Tour pro. As he mentioned on our podcast episode, "Insights on Shaving Shots off your Golf Score": *"I had a go [as a tour] player many years ago and was spectacularly unsuccessful with that. I initially went down the route of trying to search out technical perfection, which was a long, dark tunnel that I didn't really emerge from."*

That funny—and in many cases, true—anecdote is sadly representative of many golfers' attempts to improve their games and their scores. I remember what Terry Rowles told me: "Absolutes are the enemy." Though Karl Morris was unable to find technical perfection with his swing, he has an uncanny ability to demystify the psychology of practice and game improvement. His insights blow minds, change attitudes, and help golfers of all skill levels improve their performance and their enjoyment of the game.

Regarding improvement and performance, can we agree on the following: Any measurable improvement is unlikely without any practice, or at least play? Further, as my dear friend Martin Hall often says, "If you keep doing what you've been doing you'll keep getting what you've been getting." So with that said let's dive into making practice the most productive and fruitful on the course.

I contend that most golfers—even the well-informed—have an incorrect perception of how to improve. They couple success with a swing change, or lower scores with a club purchase. The real truth, as Karl says, is "surprisingly simple," and it's not some intricate swing change or technical adjustment. Karl boils it down:*"Fundamentally, you can ask two questions. When you play golf, when you're struggling, you can ask the question, 'What's wrong with my swing?' Or you can ask the question, 'What's wrong with my shots?' And if you ask the first question, you'll get a bunch of answers from a lot of different people. And a lot of that will sound really good and cool and technical ... and there will be some science thrown at you. Or you can ask the other question, 'What's wrong with the shots?' And you then start to get deep into: 'How do I produce better golf shots?' 'How can I understand what I need to do to apply the club in a certain way to produce less fade, or more draw, higher or lower [trajectory], whatever.' And I think then there can be a marvelous collaboration between the player and the coach, if it comes back to improving shots."*

I'm a firm believer that *every* practice session should be defined by a goal. That goal could be anything: a number of shots struck, a shot pattern or trajectory, a dispersion arrangement, a "feel" acquisition, a mindset or an attitude, or any combination. Successful practice begins with the end goal in mind. And while your practice shots may not be perfect, it's a successful practice session when you achieve your practice goal.

Applying that thinking to swing adjustments, any sort of technical or mechanical change is a success when the focus is on the shot produced. For example, if you're working on something, you should understand how the change will impact the journey of the golf ball. For example, if your work to shallow the shaft doesn't improve where and how the ball goes, is it really the correct thing to do? Or are you not doing it enough, or maybe are you doing it too much?

Remember, the golf course doesn't care how much you shallow the shaft in transition. It only cares if you manage to propel the golf ball to a given area or not. As Karl said, *"We always get told that golf isn't a reaction sport, and that's why it's difficult. But actually it is! Golf is a reaction sport, because you react to the images inside of your head before you step into the shot. And whatever's going through your head before the shot, you're going to react to those images. Now, I'm guessing everybody will have had those instances where the golf course has provided a situation, where there's no other option but to hit the ball low, or to curve the ball from right-to-left, or left-or-right, or whatever. And because the golf course created such a clear image in your mind of the tasks that you have to perform, that even relatively high-handicap golfers can produce some amazing shots in those situations. [It's] because they have a clear image of what they intend the shots to be, and then the body organizes around that."*

Further along in the discussion, Karl continued to emphasize the importance of visualization: *"I think building in the image of the intended shot is so important. Something that I'm so passionate about is the idea that we must be the only sport that most people who play the game are completely disconnected with the tool in their hand, with the implement that they're actually using. You know a guy playing baseball will be tuned to that bat; a cricketer is tuned to his cricket bat; a tennis player to the tennis racket. Yet, in golf, we have this huge disconnect, where we think about almost anything other than the thing that we've got in our hand. And that's paying a price for an actual evolutionary gift that we've all got, because we've evolved by using tools, by using implements, by using our hands."* Golf is a club hitting a ball—simple as that. How do you expect to play well, if you don't have any idea what the clubface is doing on every shot?

Karl galvanizes his point with a Tiger Woods example: *"The golf club ideally should be like an extension of your body. Tiger Woods is as great a player because he has such an awareness of where that golf club is in space at any given time. I love hearing him [Tiger] talk about the different shots that he played. He'll give them little names, you know, pop-ups, and stingers, and all these different kinds of names that he has for golf shots. And his ability to produce those shots comes from his awareness of where the golf club is. And you know, as Fred Shoemaker always said, 'It's far more important to know where the golf club is than where it should be.'"*

In other words, in order to better translate your practice to the golf course and have your work manifest itself into actual results, you should practice more than just technique. The addition of self-awareness and club-face awareness in space is crucial to lasting success. Even more, that emphasis coupled with skill work—such as learning to hit the ball with different trajectories, from different lies, with different clubs and in different wind conditions—will put you in the position where you will still be able to cobble together a respectable score when your swing is not on point.

When I coach and teach players, of all abilities, I begin to emphasize shot-making and creation as soon as they have a decent modicum of skill and understanding of how to hit the ball. I also recommend playing the ball from different lies, because, as you well know, that ball tends to find some awkward spots and lies. My hero, Bobby Jones, recommended that learning to play the ball down was one of the quickest ways to improve. And if Bobby Jones said so, it's gospel truth.

I also challenge players to create draws and fades around obstacles, and high and low shots over and under obstacles. In so doing, the player develops an awareness of clubface orientation in relation to the swing path and how the face must be oriented to create the desired shot. This builds confidence and empowers golfers to be able to create shots while on-course, instead of being one-dimensional, inflexible, and unable to extricate themselves from a pickle. An added benefit of this shot-making practice is that learning to hit a draw quells a fade, and learning to hit a fade mitigates a draw. So basically, while on course, instead of being a bundle of swing thoughts and theories, you can straighten shots and gain control by knowing how to hit draws and fades.

Morris urges people to keep things simple. He says, *"It's stripping away some of the complexity of the game...'* *we're drowning in information, but searching for wisdom.'"* Remembering that it's you, a club, and a ball can help you stay focused on the essentials and the basics.

Karl offered further insights on productive shot-focused, self-awareness practice with this interesting take and putting drill: *"If you think about how a baby learns to walk: the baby learns to walk not by getting it right, but by actually feeling either side of what's right. So they fall to the left, to the right, they fall forward, they fall backwards. So they gain an awareness of where they are in space, as a result of ... 'mistakes.' (They are not mistakes, they're just experiences that build a map that they respond to.) If you relate that to golf, everybody's just trying to get it right. And we don't learn by getting it right, we actually learn much better by feeling either side of what's right. So for instance ... on the putting greens, instead of trying to stand there and hole a bunch of putts, why don't you see if you can you can hit a ball that finishes to the right of the hole, then the ball that finishes to the left of the hole? Can you leave it short? Can you knock it just a foot past? And all of those things that you do in that way of learning are far more interesting, and you'd be much more engaged with it. But actually what that does is create a great learning environment where you become again tuned into the putter in your hand. What do I need to do with this putter to make it go to the right, to the left, long, short: all of those things? And then that learning is not about getting it right, it's about creating an experience that facilitates you learning how to put the ball into the hole."* It seems so simple, right? Well, the truth is that it is. This practice helps to create feel and control, as well as consistency. And those three things create confidence.

I believe golf is a game of recovery and a game of spin. You have 14 clubs, and for you, each one is designed to propel height and distance, and spin a golf ball a certain amount; they all have a purpose, can do certain things, and you have the ability to multiply each club's purpose as long as you develop an awareness of how you move and how you interact with the club. You may have 14 clubs, but on the golf course, you should have many more than 14 shots in your bag.

Are you ever confused when pros talk about *feels*? They're basically talking about being able to feel the club and the body throughout the swing, and how different kinds of swings feel. It's training your body to use and control the one tool you have—the club—to get the ball going where you want it to go. Feel is an *awareness*. Karl recommends a simple exercise to develop and enhance this awareness: *"Simply place your attention on the back-edge of your wedge. Imagine that the back edge of the wedge is the wheels of an airplane. And basically, you've got three options, there are three possible ways that you can land the plane. You can either have a nosedive where the plane smashes into the tarmac, so that's the leading edge going down to the ground. You can have an aborted landing, where the plane is coming down, but at the last minute, the pilot pulls upwards, and that's where you skull it across the green. Or you can have a smooth landing. Here's the trick with this exercise: you go out there, not with the intention of correcting anything, but just to simply hit a bunch of shots. And all you're trying to do—all you're aiming to do—is to just observe which of the three landings that you got. So you actually play a shot, and you observe what you do. Did you get a crash landing? Did you get an aborted landing, or did the back-edge of the club smoothly touch the tarmac? And just by doing it as an awareness exercise—I guarantee that 99% of people who are listening to this— your body will start to find out how to land that plane correctly."* It's the kind of curiosity and awareness that brings real improvement to propelling that ball well with that club.

In my teaching experience, that *awareness mode* is something that is sorely lacking with most amateur golfers. Often, any sort of practice involves aimless, purposeless whacking of shots or hitting of putts, which all too often results in frustration and despair. The natural response to this is to gravitate toward what Karl Morris calls the *trying mode*. That trying mode has the practicer trying to land the club perfectly instead of just being aware of how it is landing. Then when they don't achieve that, they go search for answers in all of the wrong places: ill-founded counsel or tips from a friend. In the end, the practice becomes a waste of time.

I'd recommend learning awareness of self and of the golf club, and how it is moving through space, especially at the lowest point in the swing. Where is it landing? How is it landing? Where is it swinging toward? How fast it going? Do this without hitting a golf ball until you're consistent: then you can add a golf ball to the equation.

When I'm on assignment at a PGA tournament, every time I see one of those highly talented pros face a tough, demanding lie, I always see them rehearse the base of the swing arc a few times before they strike the ball. They want to see where the club will bottom out, based on the lie and their stance. It's basically the mindset of creating the swing arc, ensuring consistency in the impact zone, so that when the ball is struck—it is not by hitting at it, but by the ball being *collected* by the clubface traveling along its arc. Simply put, they're making their very best efforts to strike the ball as solidly as possible, which involves knowing where the clubface is going, and how it'll meet the ball. It's a goal that will make every golfer better.

Karl Morris is a fascinating listen and has a wonderful way of making complex concepts easy to grasp and easier to apply. It's no wonder that he has helped countless golfers to perform at their best. And as far as performance on the golf course goes, it'll be worth your while to pay heed to this goal-setting insight: *"Decide the golfer that you're going to be on the golf course, before you play. The outcomes—the shots, the birdies and the pars—they're always going to be inconsistent. No-body in the history of the game can control that. But you can actually control the person that you are on the golf course."* I'm hearing echoes of what Nick Price and Fred Couples told me about their perspective during compet-itive rounds: it requires patience, knowing when to at-tack, and how to accept a bad shot or score and move on. Karl continues to explain the importance of being yourself and deciding how you'll react to certain out-comes, and sticking to it: *"If you decide that you're go-ing to be that resilient person, or you're going to be a person who actually enjoys the challenge, or whatever it may be that you decide, you can then stay with that for [those] 18 holes. And if you if you get to the end of the road, and you've stayed with your commitment, you can look yourself in the mirror and say, 'wow, I actually stuck with that.' Now you may or may not have produced a good score on the day, but you've stuck with the thing you said you were going to do."* And if you stick to your plan, that's a success, and success builds. If you do that more often, it will build a fantastic awareness of self, and you will be happy with the results.

I would say never forget yourself, and never get caught up in other people's wishes [or] expectations. Continue to choose your path, be the CEO of your journey. And never ever fall victim to everybody else's wishes. You can't make everybody else's life happy.

Hal Sutton

12

Hal Sutton

HARD WORK IS THE SEPARATOR

Born and raised in the hardscrabble landscape of Shreveport, Louisiana, Hal Sutton is the epitome of hard work, dedication, and sacrifice. The 1983 PGA Champion and Player of the Year rose to the top of the game, suffered through a notable slump and then—through his winning mindset and willingness to work hard and sacrifice—ascended back to the upper reaches of the PGA Tour. His second act culminated with an emphatic head-to-head triumph over Tiger Woods at the 2000 Players Championship at TPC Sawgrass. Who could ever forget the steely-eyed, determined gladiator striping a 6-iron at the flag on the 72nd hole and barking, "be the right club today"?

Sutton is a legend, and spending time in his company is always entertaining and enlightening. It was thrilling to have Hal on the podcast, and I hung on to every word he uttered in his rich Bayou accent. From the very top of our talk, Hal did not mince any words. He referenced how he chose golf over other team sports because it was an individual sport. He said he felt like he was going to work hard, and he didn't know if prospective teammates would make the same investments. He wanted the onus to be on him, and him alone. Hal shared his view of hard work: *"Work is what makes a difference. You can't buy your way into this. ... And, you know, for the most part, I'm not sure the world completely embraces that. They don't really know what that means. And I mean, I considered myself a blue-collar worker. I couldn't get anybody to do the work for me. I had to do it! You know, in the July and August months, it was hot. I'd go home to Shreveport, and I'd hit five and six hundred balls a day, I wouldn't have a dry thread on me."* I'd love any and every aspirant golfer to really consider that insight. In my 40-odd years in the game—as a competitor, a teacher, a broadcaster and now a parent—I've never seen a golfer stumble into success and improvement. It just doesn't happen. The uncomfortable truth—which Sutton has no qualms about addressing—is that work is the separator between success and failure. I am reminded of the quotation by high school basketball coach Tim Notke: "Hard work beats talent when talent doesn't work hard." And after 20+ years as a college golf coach, I can unequivocally say that hard work will beat talent every time.

The advancements in club technology have been dramatic in the past 20 years, and Sutton has seen this trend lead many golfers to try fixing their swing troubles quickly with their wallets. He puts it this way: *"Honestly, we live in a lazy world. You know, people want something for nothing. And if I can buy a driver that will fix what I want to do, well, then I'll do that. I'll spend $700 on the new driver to do that. If I can get a new set of irons and that's going to make me better, then I'll do that too. But the truth of the matter is, equipment will* never *make someone better. Work will make you better."* It's easy to blame other things and take the easy way out—throw money at the problem with a new shiny toy—than face the music and put in the hard work, on your game.

You may think that you need some innate talent to make the leap into great golf, but that's another common rationalization to avoid the necessary hard work. There's the rare occasion that a golfer's talent can accelerate improvement—and perhaps turn into a win or two—but that kind of success that won't last long. The higher you climb in competitive golf, the more you will find that plain old hard work becoming *the* separator. I have seen many talented golfers have unrequited, frustrating times, while I have seen many less-talented players—who have put in the work—thrive and excel.

Now, when you're working hard, you need to ensure that you're working on the right thing. It would be a fool's errand to go and chop down a tree without knowing which tree requires chopping. In golf, if you work on the wrong thing, you can get *further* away from improvement, while wasting a lot of time. So find yourself a knowledgeable and trustworthy coach and/or mentor. Hal Sutton did so, and he was fortunate enough to find a hall-of-famer as a source of counsel. Hal recalls in his early career, *"I finished [as] Rookie of the Year, and the first six months I didn't do any good. I was traveling and didn't really know how to play the tour. And Raymond Floyd took me under his wing and began to play with me every Tuesday, and he showed me how to play professional golf. He taught me you've got to learn how to hit it pin-high, every shot."* There's basically four ways to miss: left and right, but also short and long. If you learn how to control your distance, by way of truly knowing how far you hit the ball, proper club selection and solid contact, you're eliminating two of those right away.

For what it's worth, Hal also counts Byron Nelson and Ben Hogan as mentors. I mean, what a thrill. Learning, as a young man, from a true statesman of the game in Nelson, and from one of the great swingers of all time in Hogan, and then as a rookie professional spending time under the advice of arguably one of the PGA Tour's greatest competitors in Ray Floyd: incredible! To Sutton's credit, he took every one of the lessons he learned and applied them to his craft. Therein is another important lesson: don't be that person who gets credible advice, or takes a lesson, only to abandon it when the going gets tough. Be resilient, work hard, and stick to it, because improvement is slow, incremental, and non-linear in progression. There are inevitable ups and downs. If you can improve just a little bit every day, you'll notice a marked improvement sooner than you think.

That all being said, Hal realized that he could not be Byron, or Ben, or Raymond. He could only be himself. He could most certainly take the lessons he learned, but he had to make them personal, so he was able to perform at his best as often as possible. Like young Collin Morikawa, Sutton also quickly learned that handling pressure and expectations were an unwritten key to success.

After beating his boyhood idol, Jack Nicklaus, at Riviera to win the 1983 PGA Championship, the golf world heaped the inevitable high expectations on him. His response was one that all golfers can learn from: *"To get those sorts of accolades put on you early on was extra pressure. You know, I played golf for me, I didn't play golf for the rest of the world. And, you know, I had my own expectations."* There's a recurring theme: Shut out the noise and follow your own personal goals.

Now even Hal Sutton was not bullet-proof enough to be immune to it all. He did get frustrated with the public's unreasonable expectations, and it pushed him away from the game a bit. But in typical Hal Sutton fashion, he bounced back. His mantra is one that he'd offer as advice to any aspirant golfer: *"I would say never forget yourself, and never get caught up in other people's wishes [and] expectations. Continue to choose your path, be the CEO of your journey. And never, ever fall victim to everybody else's wishes. You can't make everybody else's life happy, there's no way."* He then elaborated, *"so if I have any advice for everybody out there, you determine who you are and who you want to be. You make the decisions that help you get to where you want to go. Don't let others that really don't know influence that."* It's remarkable how much Hal's advice echoes those made by Nick Price, Fred Couples, and Collin Morikawa. If it worked for these four rather different players, it could certainly work for you.

Sutton also possesses the unique ability to strip the game down to its nuts and bolts. Consider these nuggets and the lessons embedded in them. Hal explains that he learned to keep his thinking simple and straightforward, and it serves as a reminder to us all: *"the 7-iron that you hit with your buddies at home, it's the same 7-iron that you would hit on the last shot of the day, against the best player in the world. And truthfully, that's what that came down to. Yeah, just make it that simple! Then you can perform at the highest level under the most pressure."* What a wonderfully simple—yet stunningly profound—observation. No matter how important—or difficult, or daunting, or even easy—the upcoming shot is, it's really just another 7-iron, or drive, or wedge. The mechanics of the shot do not change: what differs is the moment, the pressure, and the corresponding emotional and mental challenges. Try to make high-pressure situations feel like a moment with your friends. After all, it's the same ball, and the same club: why not the same swing and result?

I believe the elite tournament golfer is able to separate the emotions of golf from the physical mechanics. When asked about an important upcoming round, I've heard countless PGA Tour pros respond, "I'm just going to try and take it like any other round." Even though that's easier said than done, and very difficult to actually accomplish, this approach can create the requisite mindset and attitude.

The faster you can get to a strong sense of self, and to forget the noise and expectations, the better off you'll be. Hal puts it this way: *"At 62 years old, you kind of define who you are, you become comfortable in who you are. If [you] could get to that point when [you're] 22, boy, [you'll] really accomplish things. Because then you're not driven for anything except the honesty, the truth in light of who you are."*

Hal Sutton is an American treasure. At this point, you should download and listen to the podcast with Hal. His mental game is bar none, shaped by the fantastic advice of his legendary mentors and built like a fortress to defend against the challenges of competitive golf. He's an achiever at the highest level who has remained true to himself and his Southern roots. He is, in my opinion, the embodiment of honesty, fortitude, and savvy. He's a rugged individual, a perpetual grinder, and a gladiator who's truly comfortable in his own skin. This 14-time PGA Tour winner—who learned so much from Nelson, Hogan, and Floyd, and from his own sweat—knows what he's talking about.

No two people are built the same and so it's a fool's errand to teach them the same way.

Terry Rowles

13

Terry Rowles

THE BEST VERSION OF YOURSELF

Terry Rowles is possibly the most underrated teacher in the game. I believe he's in a league above most of his peers. Despite his accolades—*Golf Digest* 50 Best Teachers in America and *Golf Magazine* Top 100 Teachers in America—I believe his renown should be a whole lot greater.

Terry's mind is incisive, and with his expertise in club-fitting and 3D swing measurement, he brings an all-encompassing level of know-how to every lesson he gives. Such is my respect for his intellect that he has made three appearances on my *On the Mark* podcast, and each time he has been thoroughly entertaining and very informational.

Based in the United States, but originally from southwest England, the Cornwall native speaks with great authority on a variety of swing concepts but—thanks to extensive research—Rowles specializes in the grip and its effect on movement, and in how players can use the shift in mass to maximize power. He shared a credo that has become a recurring message of this book. In Terry's words, *"No two people are built the same, and so it's a fool's errand to teach them the same way."* It should be the guiding light of all teachers, as well as students who are seeking a teacher.

He also believes that golfers need to proceed with caution when making swing changes. Terry explains, *"The first thing to do when you look at a thing you don't like in your own golf swing be that in a video, or in 3D, is to say, 'Is that doing something good for me?'"* Watching your swing videos can be a bit awkward and disheartening, like hearing a recording of your own voice. But everyone feels that way.

The truth is, armed with a phone that can video their own swings, golfers tend to want to change things that don't look "nice" or "correct." This tendency toward aesthetic improvement is a dangerous and potentially a game-wrecking mentality, as the golf swing is—as Terry calls it—a mechanism in which *"everything has an effect on steepeners and shallowers, on opening and closing the face, on generating speed, on hitting the ground in the right place. There's just a ton of things that are really important that you match up and balance in a golf swing."* He quickly added this advice: *"Be weary when you're making swing changes, because the thing that doesn't look right might be the perfect matchup that makes you play well three times out of four."* Rowles' approach naturally sets the challenge to find out what makes your swing work instead of finding the things that are breaking it down.

Before we dive into Terry's explanations—rooted in technology and his 3D research—on how to create speed and power, I'd like to talk about another axiom of Terry's: *"Absolutes are the enemy."* As the podcast host, it's my job to introduce the guest and guide him or her to a place where they unveil their knowledge and expertise, share insights, tips and takes, and help listeners to a better understanding of concepts so they may advance to a place of understanding. By *understanding*, I mean when the student understands a concept enough to make their own informed and calculated decisions and eventually becomes the master of their own destiny. I sometimes have to ask questions with a generic bent, as my podcast has a wide-ranging spectrum of listeners, from beginners to elite players. Rest assured, the last thing I want is for some aspirant golfer to listen to my show and misunderstand and misapply something, as it could have disastrous consequences. And I *don't* want to be the author of that story.

Terry is correct: absolutes are the enemy, and we can apply that truism to everything in life and certainly everything in the golf swing. As it pertains to power off the tee, Terry did make a few statements about the physics of the swing that certainly are, in my opinion, crucial to understand: *"All the clubhead speed in the world amounts to nothing if it doesn't parlay into added distance off the tee."* Swinging the club upwards of 120 mph (for example) and making contact far from the center of the clubface—or hitting the shot into the words and out-of-bounds—amount to nothing but a worse score. I'd much rather have 110 mph struck squarely and in play, than 120 mph and in trouble or out of play. See what I mean?

Rowles also explains that *"power is the combination of strength and speed."* Rarely is a physically weak golfer a power-hitter. You don't have to be exceptionally tall or bulky to be a bomber, but all bombers are strong and fast. Justin Thomas and Will Zalatoris are slightly built, but they are very strong, and very fast. If you want to hit the ball farther, you must get stronger to get faster. The good news is that you can often work on these two goals at the same time.

And his third observation, as it relates to power:

"The clubhead is traveling a greater distance than the hands, and the hands are traveling farther than the shoulders, because of the orbital nature of the golf swing." The golf swing is a three-dimensional arc, and a number of different elements are moving in arcs around the body. A key to success is to get those elements moving in time with each other. The term, therefore, is proper kinematic sequencing. And I'll always remember when I asked Nick Faldo what the most important thing in the swing is and he said, "the clubhead has the furthest journey to travel; makes sure it moves the most." All too often I see golfers trying to gain more speed and power by simply improving their pivot, or their footwork. This approach is devoid of logic if it is not complemented by a purposeful acceleration of the arms and hands as well.

Rowles then made an important insight about power—and though it sounds obvious, it's often overlooked by many a golfer: *"What we usually find with the longest hitters is that they don't have a restricted swing."* A powerful swing results from the body having permission to move freely. He went further by explaining his—and Mike Adams'—approach to power off the tee. (Recall Adams' quotation on when power should be added to the equation.) Terry says that there are *"two different types of instruction theory. One is called 'inhibitors' where people put towels under the arms, and they restrict their hip rotation, you know keep the left foot on the ground versus 'accelerators.'"*

Terry maintains that if anyone goes for a lesson with him, he'll always find and work on a motion or a force application, which is a positive way solving the problem. In other words, most golfers should not be restricting movement for improvement, especially when it comes to building up speed. The reason being is that the majority of amateur golfers do not have the physical capability of producing speed over a short space of time. There are the obvious outliers with shorter, more compact swings—like Jon Rahm—but Rowles used the example of Bryson DeChambeau's swing, which changed from a geometrically sound-yet-inhibited swing to an uninhibited motion that gave him more time to generate speed. His results were massive, and they spurned a trend on the PGA Tour. Terry continued, *"Adding motion is a good thing; that's not the reason people hit it off-line. The hit is off-line because they have bad ball-position, they have bad aim, the grip is wrong, not because they have a long swing. If you have a bad grip, bad aim, and you make your swing shorter, you just have a shorter, shitty golf game."*

As Terry shared that gem I giggled—thanks to his use of the highly technical golf term "shitty"—and mentioned something to the effect of, "you're preaching, Reverend Rowles." Indeed, his message is gospel truth. It brings to mind my list of those generic golf tips that everybody has and distributes for all manner of swing ailments: "Band-Aids for the golf swing." The list includes "keep your head down," which incidentally I heard too often while playing in a pro-am recently. But I digress. What goes unsaid in that Rowles' observation is that in most cases, swing mistakes happen before the golf club is even swung. So that's the place where Terry Rowles largely operates.

He is a stickler about the grip, ball position, and weight shift, relative to the way the golf club is held. Terry says, *"The grip has an effect on how much the pelvis sways toward the target."* In other words, holding the club in a certain manner and then trying to work on a pivot and body movement that doesn't support that grip, and its effect on the clubface is unlikely to be good. Rowles essentially explained the relationship as follows: *"the lead hand is relative to the type of pivot that you have, so if you're somebody that opens up faster and more, then the handle is gonna be more forward, so you're gonna need a stronger left hand. So the left hand is matched up to your pivot; the right hand is to control the clubface (in a non-conscious way)."*

Basically, a stronger lead-hand grip, where the club is held more in the fingers and the hand is turned more onto the top of the grip with the glove-logo visible, is going to manifest in a more closed clubface, likely to produce a pull, draw, hook, or pull hook. As a result, a more active and faster body pivot and shift is required to mitigate that tendency and send the ball straighter. This is why the majority of elite golfers grip the club with a stronger lead hand, as that style requires a faster body action. Or on the flipside of the statement, a faster body action—for added clubhead speed—requires a more closed clubface in order to keep shots from veering off to the weak side. And purely for informational sake, this was not the case back in the day: Jack Nicklaus, for example, who was a power-hitter, held the club with a grip that was much weaker than modern-day bombers like Rory McIlroy or Dustin Johnson.

Conversely, a weaker grip—with the top hand turned more to the side, or even underneath the club—is going to promote an open clubface, which will direct golf shots toward the weak side of the target line (a fade or slice). Hence, to square the shot up, a more passive body-rotation and shift is necessary.

Incidentally Terry breaks the styles of backswing pivot into three types: front post, center post, and rear post. To understand these pivot types, imagine your legs are posts. Certain golfers rotate around the front leg; some rotate around the center (with a slight movement to the trail side), and some golfers move completely to the back leg. Each way works, but this movement has to be supported by—and must complement—the grip style.

Terry did qualify that the shift of pressure and

weight is a widely misunderstood concept: *"One of the big misconceptions of getting speed is you have to move more to the right [trail side], and it's a relatively small number of people that will potentially get better doing that."* In other words, too many golfers shift to the rear post too much, and for too long, and that makes it very hard to rotate powerfully through contact without the path of the club being compromised. Further, as it relates to speed and power, the corresponding lateral shift back to the target reduces the chances of "cracking of the whip": allowing the clubhead to be slingshot off the pivot of the torso for an extra burst of speed. It's basically why you can hit the ball, with your feet placed together, nearly as far as your full swing with your regular stance. With your feet touching each other, your pivot is stabilized and centralized, and the transfer of energy from the pivot to the club is more efficient and timed.

So, for better contact and power, settle on your grip before you work on your body action. Or at least identify how your grip influences the clubface, in terms of being open or closed, before you work on the body pivot and exploiting ground reaction forces. As Terry advised: *"It's a complete fool's errand to try and use the style of ground force that is not yours."*

Terry Rowles is a master instructor and swing coach. In his own words: *"My greatest pleasure is helping golfers overcome slumps and becoming the best version of themselves. There is a way to become the golfer you think you are."* Much of improving your game involves knowing you are, what your body likes to do and is capable of, and letting everything work together. So if your teacher talks a lot about grip, don't think they think you're a beginner. It's because what happens before the swing makes the biggest difference.

I ask myself the question, 'How do I get better while working less?' And when you think about different scenarios you start to realize the most efficient answer—Occam's razor—sometimes the simplest answer is the best answer.

Bryson DeChambeau

14

Bryson DeChambeau

LEAVING NO STONE UNTURNED

Love him or hate him, Bryson DeChambeau loves golf and loves figuring out new approaches and solutions to our great game. In his own way, the former U.S. Amateur and U.S. Open Champion was the genesis of an arms race in the professional game. He's talented, candid, well-read, opinionated, and not afraid of disagreement or confrontation. Bryson DeChambeau is more than just a talented golfer, he's a personality and an entertainer.

My in-person conversation with Bryson for my podcast was both thoroughly entertaining and vastly informative. He really is like a kid in a candy store when it comes to golf, the golf swing, and game improvement, and his energy and passion are palpable. He explained his general approach this way: *"I'll give you a good little insight into how I work. I literally go down any road possible to get better, but I always have a baseline. I've got a rope attached to me, so when I go down rabbit holes, I'm able to get pulled out."*

What DeChambeau says here is loaded with insights and advice that can benefit golfers of all abilities. Go out to the practice facility and like Bryson, try different things. As Ben Hogan once said, all of us must *"dig it out of the dirt."* Experiment, try different things; don't worry what others may think of you. However, do maintain a keen knowledge and awareness of where your baseline is—what your swing today accomplishes, in terms of distance, accuracy, spin, and so on—whether you discover it by video, launch monitor data, feel, or all three. Then you can go searching for different ways to improve. Who knows what you might find? Bryson adds, *"Sometimes the best discovery is self-discovery. You learn the most from self-discovery, and that's where he [Bryson's coach Mike Schy] wanted me to fail as much as possible, as quickly as possible, so that I could find the most effective path in a quick amount of time."* I really appreciate the willingness to push yourself and being open to failure; if you want to improve at anything, these two qualities are essential. And failures often lead to future improvements and successes.

Though he is a somewhat polarizing figure, you can't help but respect DeChambeau and his intense desire to improve himself and his game. Bryson is prepared to go to lengths that most people would never even consider. My goodness, he famously changed his entire physique to generate more clubhead speed and power. His process of improvement starts with thinking outside of the box, remembering that simplicity is a good thing, and asking worthwhile questions is equally important: *"I ask myself the question, 'How do I get better while working less?' And when you think about different scenarios you start to realize the most efficient answer—Occam's razor—sometimes the simplest answer is the best answer."*

It's hard to fathom that for all of the scientific speak, Bryson is indeed simplistic in his ways. He's always just trying to find the most efficient way to get the best out of himself. And I credit him for this wise approach, because all too often aspirant (and sometimes desperate) golfers just go ahead and try any old thing to somehow hit the ball straighter or make more putts. Sadly, in many cases, they embark on journeys where their brains write checks that their bodies cannot cash.

Not DeChambeau. Bryson recalls an iconic statement: *"Just like Arnold [Palmer] said, 'swing your swing.' I take that to heart."* The complete version is: *"Swing your swing, not some idea of the swing. Not a swing you saw on TV. Not that swing you wish you had. No, swing your swing."* Naturally, I wholeheartedly agree with The King, but Bryson and I also advocate that golfers find more efficient and productive ways to propel the golf ball to its destination. And obviously if a swing isn't productive and not consistent, then adjustments need to be made. Whatever the reason, swing adjustments should fit into your physical abilities to produce and sustain and duplicate them. Anything beyond those limitations isn't "swinging your swing."

Once you have resolved to make a change in technique, you have to commit time to reprogramming your mind, motor habits, and movement patterns. In order for true, lasting development to occur, intent, focus, and plain old hard work is required. No lip-service, no practice once-in-a-while. Just consistent hard work. Even the very best players with the best physical abilities practice a lot, so if you want to make an improvement, why would you think you'd get away with any less? Bryson recalls the work ethic of a golfer he admires: *"I'll tell you this, and Kyle [Berkshire] said this before. Leading up to Worlds [Long-Driving Championship] he was hitting approximately 600 balls a day with a driver, full-out. Three speed-training sessions almost every day."* Kyle Berkshire's speed-work blows my mind. A regimen of 600 balls a day is incredible, and 600 drivers at maximum speed is downright unfathomable.

It's certainly not doable for anyone other than Kyle, but the dedication and devotion and discipline are what I want you to register here.

Remember that the dedication, devotion, and discipline also come with a little pain, which you can and must endure if you are serious about change. Bryson explains, *"Sometimes when you're sore, when your hands are hurting, when your body is hurting, you just gotta push through when you're speed training, because it's not about training the muscular structure. It's about training the nervous system to fire faster."* This insight touches on two aspects of game improvement: power, which I will address shortly, and resilience. Resilience—or toughness, or 'stick-to-it-iveness'—is a personality trait common to every great golfer I've ever met. Golf is tough. It's simple, but it's not easy, and change takes time. (Recall the Tiger Woods quip from Butch Harmon.) Improvement doesn't happen overnight, and the folks who have built long-lasting habits are the ones who have had the wherewithal to stick to the task at hand, through thick and thin. Bryson states, *"I mean yes, there is probably better moments in your body's life span that can enhance the ability, but everybody can get faster if they really put their mind to it."*

So, back to the power off the tee. Something everybody wants. DeChambeau went from an above average to a super-long hitter by basically getting heavier and much stronger, and swinging longer and much faster. Certainly, his specific approach wouldn't work for most of us, but the principle will: Safe speed training is highly beneficial, because you won't hit the ball any farther unless you increase clubhead speed and as a result ball speed.

In my many years as a teacher, I have encountered golfers who got longer—but also got wilder—off the tee. Consequently, their scores didn't improve. DeChambeau, believe it or not, took the opposite tack: *"I built a golf swing to go straight first, hit it as straight as possible, and then I'm adding speed to it, continuously adding speed.*" That is wise advice for everyone. Remember length off the tee is only an advantage if it turns into lower scores—unless of course you want to get into long-drive contests. Let's remember that a 250-yard drive in the fairway is much better than 300 yards into a hazard or penalty area.

Swing speed is a catalyst for ball speed, which is the real goal. Increasing your *clubhead speed* dramatically will not amount to any distance gains if it doesn't translate into higher, more efficient *ball speed* and aerodynamics. I spoke with a technician and ballistics expert from FlightScope, and he shared the following: "*ball speed is the best contributor to distance. A player swinging at 115-mph [clubhead speed] with a 1.5 smash factor is much better off than a 125-mph player who ranges between 1.4 and 1.45 smash factor numbers. One can then assume the 125-mph player has many more off-center hits, which don't just affect his distance, but also his dispersion.*"

In this example, *smash factor* is the measurement of the quality of the strike. Smash factor is calculated by dividing the ball speed by the clubhead speed. As an example, if you swing a driver with a clubhead speed of 100 mph and it generates a ball speed of 150 mph, the smash factor will be 1.50. In other words, the higher the smash factor value, the more ball speed will be obtained for any given clubhead speed. Typically, launch monitors give smash-factor values that range between 1.3 and 1.4 with a 7-iron, and 1.44 to 1.52 with a driver. So it's not exactly how fast you swing the club, it's how fast you make the ball go.

Generating strong clubhead speed requires various factors to occur, and all of those should point toward an improved transfer of energy from the swinger into the club. Bryson originally focused on just going harder with more mass. Eventually, after connecting with World Long-Driving Champion, Kyle Berkshire, he modified his approach to put less strain on his body. He pivoted from violently bludgeoning the ball to creating a more efficient, athletic move that wound up and then released speed. He began to hone in on improving the timing of the moving parts in the swing: *"In kinematics, in order to create the most velocity at a certain point in time, you have to have time to accelerate in distance. You could have a huge engine, get there really quickly, but that's under a shorter amount of distance, or you can get there by a super-long swing, applying the same acceleration to it. So you want something that has the same acceleration."*

I responded to Bryson with an illustrative simile: comparing two NASCAR tracks—Talladega and Bristol Motor Speedways—with the same car driving around them. I said that the top speeds are significantly higher at Talladega than at Bristol, and it's because Talladega is about 2.6 miles long, and Bristol is just over a half a mile long. He responded to the comparison: *"When people swing smooth and take it a little bit longer back and take more time at the top, that gives them the ability to accelerate the club through the stretch-shortening cycle a lot more efficiently and they can hit it farther."*

What's a stretch-shortening cycle, you may ask? Simply put, it refers to the muscle action when active muscle lengthening precedes active muscle shortening. It's basically a counter-movement, during which the muscles involved are first stretched and then shortened to accelerate the body or a limb. A good example of it is how Kyle Berkshire looks like he "stands up" in the backswing, and then lowers toward the ground in transition as leverage to "push up" with his legs through impact into the finish. While that cycle is a valuable part in generating energy and leverage for added club-head speed, it's not the only element involved. Bryson expanded on how to create more speed: *"You have to take a longer, softer, wider swing, and if you can do that, and load the wrists, and then unload it, and stay tall through impact. Don't shrink down ... stay tall. That increases the lever length and then you can rip the club a lot faster."*

On the heels of that beautiful description of how to generate more physical speed, I want to pivot (pun intended) back to the mindset and the power of the mind. Bryson once made this statement in a press conference, which resonated so much with me that I transcribed and saved it: *"If you can believe in it at the fullest level, everything else doesn't matter."* I spoke with DeChambeau during a practice round at the 2022 PGA Championship. He was returning to action after being sidelined due to wrist injury a few months prior. I asked about the surgery, his recovery, and how much practice he managed to get in before the event. Bryson emphatically shared that his practice had been minimal. My follow-up question involved how he had managed to return with his swing being so sharp. He responded by explaining that he'd practice by sitting in a chair as he visualized his perfect golf swing. He would visualize and "feel" exactly what he wanted to do. As he did that mental practice, he would prime his body for performance when he returned to action. Such is the power of DeChambeau's belief.

In fact, after he won the 2020 U.S. Open at Winged Foot with a virtuoso performance that for all intents and purposes decimated the field and the golf course, I posted a message on social media: "Bryson DeChambeau, Congratulations! You made significant sacrifices to elevate your game and achieve your goals. You stayed the course despite incredible criticism and headwind. Now you are a Major Champion. Very, very well deserved." That post happened to go viral, and honestly, I'm not entirely sure why. I was really only trying to make a point and illustrate a lesson for people and golfers: whereas constructive criticism can be helpful, criticism in general is mostly hurtful and certainly detracting of focus. Much of the online criticism leveled at Bryson was hardly constructive. In fact, the Twittersphere—and a lot of golf fans— made a number of uninformed personal jabs at him. To his credit, DeChambeau focused his mind, galvanized his intent, put on his blinders, and stuck to his work. The validation for his approach was an impressive U.S. Open victory.

With all the rampant and readily available information online, it's easy to become waylaid by something new or alluring. It's tempting to pursue something you see online that's guaranteed to improve your game. The truth is that it could in face be completely inapplicable to you. Don't forget the abundance of golf "insight" available in any locker room, grill room, or driving range. Avoid this stuff! To quote Butch Harmon: *"If someone tells you there is one perfect swing, walk away, and don't listen to another word."* With all the voices and opinions out there, it's easy to get too many conflicting ideas, tips, and theories in your head. All that confusion will never help.

The power of the mind is real and not something to be scoffed at. DeChambeau has sometimes been called the Mad Scientist, but he's definitely not mad. He's thoughtful, explorative, and prepared to forge his own path. He's smart and calculated, but he also understands that there are elements to golf which can't necessarily be measured with a launch monitor or a sensor. And it's not all science for Bryson. As he shares, *"If you can beautifully mesh the art and science of it to enhance your game, there's no downside to it."*

There is a lot to learn from the Bryson: some of it physical, some of it mental, some of it emotional. Amid all the physical changes he's made, you can't underestimate the power of resilience, positivity, and self-belief. As Bryson concludes, *"Hope is always something that trumps the doubt."*

The older I get, the more I realize how lucky I am to have golf in my life. I feel like I am a very, very ordinary person who's living an extraordinary life because of the game of golf.

Bill Harmon

15

Bill Harmon

GIVE ME TOUGH OVER GOOD, ANY DAY

Bill Harmon is a national treasure. Of Claude Harmon's four sons—Butch, Craig, Dick, and Bill—youngest Bill was arguably the best golfer in the family. He is charming, funny, and wise. His wisdom and knowledge of golf is enduring, and he dispenses said wisdom in a way that makes the receiver think, and then more often than not go, "that makes so much sense."

Bill Harmon has lived an adventurous life, and I believe his odyssey has made him the wise savant that he is. Bill looked back and said, *"Because of my father [Claude] and my upbringing, I've been exposed to so many wonderful people, places, things, and experiences."* After about with alcoholism and substance abuse, Bill is recovering, sober and fiercely thankful for life and good health. What he said next has resonated with me since our podcast conversation in October 2022: *"The older I get, the more*

I realize how lucky I am to have golf in my life. I feel like I am a very, very ordinary person who's living an extraordinary life because of the game of golf. And you know, I have received so much more from the game than I could possibly give back." Bill's sentiments and his honesty uncovered something I have always known, but never been able to describe: golf is the greatest of games, and it has also blessed me beyond measure.

It's truly amazing how this timeless game—which can be so difficult, yet so rewarding—can open doors that typically could never be opened. Bill and I are living proof of that, and it's why I advocate that all young people take up golf: not just for the network it provides, but more so for the life lessons it teaches. So let's get to some life—and golf—lessons from the former PGA Tour caddie and *Golf Magazine* top-100 instructor, and a man who takes more pride in helping an amateur golfer lower his handicap than he does helping a tour pro.

As one would expect, many of Bill's insights originate from his father, Claude Harmon, who was the long-time teaching professional at Winged Foot and Seminole, and also the 1948 Masters champion. Bill recollects, *"It's funny because when I was younger, some of the pearls [of wisdom from his father] bothered me. Because he was a pathological truth-teller. And when you're 15 and 16, you don't really want to hear the truth. I now look back on them, and a lot of the things he said that I thought were irritating are actually quite funny. And actually very knowledgeable."*

Bill continued by elaborating on an axiom he learned from his father that he still applies to his lessons today: *"I think some of the things [he said] that have helped me as a teacher, one of them is: 'Show me someone who practices for today, and I'll show you someone will never get better.' You have to have vision."* Here, *vision* basically is *a plan* that includes a concrete, thought-out process and goals that will define, govern, and motivate the correct and appropriate work on whatever issues need to be addressed. But *vision* is a better word for it!

Harmon then stressed two very important elements to lasting improvement, that it be a long-term approach and that it involves more than just working on the golf swing. He recalls that his father Claude *"always felt that you should identify—let's say—your golf issues. Everyone thinks nowadays it's all in the swing, I think that's only part of it. Now you should have almost a yearly plan. You know, where do you want to be a year from now? So if you're a snap-hooker, a year from now you want to eliminate the left side of the course. If you're a bad putter, a year from now you want to make yourself an above-average putter. So you have to get involved in the process. And I think that's where a lot of golfers say they want to get better. But it's not easy to get better, because change isn't always easy in golf."*

The second axiom was about the nature of golf, and the nature of the human beings playing the game and endeavoring to play the game better. Claude Harmon posed it as a rhetorical question: *"If good golf is so easy, why aren't there more good golfers?"* Bill Harmon contends that good golf really isn't that easy. I think there are a few reasons for this. Most notably the human factor—we are all humans that play golf, right? Well, in my 25+ years of teaching and coaching the game I can categorically state that the lion's share of golfers aren't truly prepared to make the requisite sacrifices for whole-hearted and proper change. They are like the baseball players who are safely on first base, who want to steal second, but they aren't prepared to take the foot off first and venture into that uncomfortable gap between the first and second bases. You can't reach your goals—or even make progress—if you're too afraid to take the leap.

Further, change is never easy and it is typically uncomfortable. Habits are usually engrained and hard to break, and golf is a game full of habits. Bill elaborated with a personal yarn: *"And one of the things he [father] said to me early on, that I really didn't like, [was when] he changed my grip. And I said, 'well Daddy, that doesn't feel good.' And his exact words were, 'you appear to be a bright young man.' I couldn't say that I was. And he asked me if I knew what an inanimate object was. I said, 'I think so.' And he said, 'is the golf ball inanimate?' And he said, 'is the object striking the ball inanimate?' And I said, 'yes.' He said, 'those two things don't care about your feelings. The downswing is not an encounter group. The golf ball is eventually going to go where the clubface tells it to go.'"* The grip influences so much in the swing, and it's our only true connection to the club, which directly influences the ball, so grip changes are very hard and very uncomfortable. Bad habits are easy and very comfortable: that's why we keep doing them! It's through creating new habits—and replacing the old, bad ones—that we make lasting, meaningful change. What's uncomfortable at first can initiate lasting improvement.

He then quickly pivoted back to the amateur golfer—I told you giving lessons to amateur golfers was Bill's favorite thing to do: *"but when you're learning the game, my experience is that eventually the amateur golfer bottoms out with his technique. So most golfers when they take up golf, are not very good, and play and they play and they play, and let's say they get down to an 18 [handicap]. But now they're between 16 and 20 for 10 straight years, because they can't get any better. Whether it's short-game technique, or long-game technique, or the way they think, or the way they manage the course."* If your swing doesn't improve, and your practicing doesn't improve, your mindset doesn't improve, and your knowledge-base doesn't improve, then how are you expecting that your scores will improve?

Bill drew a parallel between a golfer who doesn't improve over time and a person in the workplace who never really improves or advances their skill over 10 years and how they would likely be fired if so. People can get too comfortable—some call it personally stuck— in their jobs or careers, and they can also get stuck in their swings and their scores. So fire your bad habits, or they'll continue to plague your performance.

He then delved into the nuts and bolts of true game improvement: *"As you know, change isn't easy, because we do care how we feel. And so you have to identify the areas. My late brother Dick—and this is ... for the recreational golfer, [and] I think he's 100% right—he said there's four tenets to golf: 1. Can you hit a golf ball? 2. Short game ... Part 3 and 4 we never talk about: 3. How do you manage yourself, and 4. How do you manage the hole you're playing? When I play with my members, they're so bad at Parts 3 and 4, but yet they think if they hit it five yards farther, they're gonna be better."* Many of our bad habits aren't necessary in our swing or technique, they're born in our mind and the way we think.

Harmon chortled after that remark, and then he continued on the important topic of course management. *"I think golf course management isn't taught enough at the recreational level. I had the advantage: my dad learned course management from Ben Hogan. You know what? I caddied for Jay Haas. Oddly enough ... he looked at the game almost exactly the way my father looked at the game. It was Point A to Point B experience. You had to know when hold 'em, when to fold 'em—when to shoot at pins and when not to shoot at pins—because he [Jay] didn't have the power to overcome a course. So when I caddied for Jay, it was like I was watching my father. So I think players could get much, much better: 25% better from 100 yards on in and managing the golf course better. Those two things. If they never hit another driver, another fairway wood, another hybrid [they'd be a] minimum of 25% better if they could get better from 100 yards and think a little better."* This advice sounds like what Price and Hovland did to become world elites.

I love the idea of knowing when to hold and when to fold on the golf course. Golf is basically a game of probability, just like gambling. Every shot you face has a probability of success and/or failure. Every shot you face has a risk and a reward element to it. The good gambler, and for that matter the good golfer, knows when to take a risk and he also knows when to cut his losses. We saw it in Nick Price's evolving approach to links golf, and in his advice to pay attention to the percentages—or odds—of certain shot outcomes. Before you take a chance, you should calculate the risk, and assess the possible reward. Weigh the two up against each other and make a disciplined and smart decision.

To me I feel like this skill of knowing the probability of success—and also knowing what success represents—is one that a precious few golfers possess. Even worse, it's a skill that almost no golfers ever apply. In terms of whether to hold and when to fold, you can't just avoid hitting the shot at all, but you can pick a shot that you know the chances of success are measurably more than the chances of failure.

Nick Faldo once told me his way of assessing shots under pressure. In his conversations with his long-time caddie, Fanny Suneson, after all of the necessary info about an on-course situation was obtained—such as the lie, the wind, the pin location, the yardages, the hazards—Nick and Fanny would answer two questions: "What do I want?" and "What can I do?"

The shot that Sir Nick would choose to hit would be the one that accommodated both answers. For example, if Nick had a 200-yard shot over water to a tucked flag, he would ask the two questions. Naturally he would want to hit it at the flag, but if his swing didn't feel good, or if the wind was blustery and unpredictable, or if he was unsure he could pull the shot off, or add any other variable that reduced the chance of success, he would move his target to the safe side of the flag. Then he re-asked the questions, the chances of his *want* and his *can-do*, and saw if they moved closer to each other. If they did not, he would move his target once more. If in fact the *want* and the *can-do* did intersected, then that became the shot that he was going to hit. The habit of answering these two questions led Faldo to become a masterful tactician, winning multiple majors at true strategic championship courses, at Augusta National, the Old Course at St Andrews, and Muirfield. In fact, his judicious shot selection and risk-avoidance famously allowed Nick to make 18 pars in the final round of the 1987 Open at Muirfield, when the rest of the leaderboard made tactical mistakes down the stretch.

Go ahead and play nine holes using Nick and Fanny's two questions. You'll be pleasantly surprised how it'll reduce the amount of big numbers on your scorecard.

One thing about course management, though, is that it requires a level of brutal honesty for it to be successful. Put in another way: if you're living in a fool's paradise and your assessment of your skills and your know-how are amiss, there's little chance that you'll ever make smart and successful course management decisions. You have to know yourself. Think of Harmon's term, "a pathological truth-teller": that's what you have to be with yourself. And remember that if someone as good and as precise a ball-striker as Faldo sometimes felt like he couldn't pull off a shot—that the risk or odds were too great, the percentages too bad—then no one in the world can pull off every shot they want. Knowing your tendencies, your limits, your habits—there's that word again—leads to true self-knowledge on the course, and only then can you make sound decisions.

This is the perfect segue to Harmon's observation of golf being a "Point A to Point B experience." Obviously, Point A is not always the middle of the fairway, and Point B is not always the hole. We would love it to be, but it just is not. Building on that, most folks get on the tee and swing like they are trying to swing for Point B, instead of Point A, and disaster becomes inevitable.

Further, most golfers just feel like the first shot has to be with a driver, even though their driver may be the most inconsistent club in their bag. Their habit is not to think about probabilities: they just roll the dice and hope. Let's say their chance of success is 25%, which means they have a 3-in-4 chance of failure. They try the shot anyway, and the probability is brought to bear, and they end up hitting the ball to Point Z instead of Point B.

You can't spell *probability* without *probably*. Harmon said something you *probably* didn't really pay attention to: *"If they [amateur golfers] never hit another driver, another fairway wood, another hybrid, [they would improve] a minimum of 25%."* Bill isn't implying that a golfer is likely to make more birdies by avoiding the driver off the tee. What he does mean is that a golfer will most surely avoid more double bogeys and worse by keeping the ball in play. The change would eliminate the downside, improve the probability ... probably.

Now I recognize that strokes-gained-off-the-tee metric proves that longer drives enhance the probability of better approach shots. Indeed, when you have a wide fairway, and your Nick Faldo *wants* and *can-do's* intersect, go ahead and swing away. If, however, your target landing area is small and riddled with hazards, and you have no idea where you next driver is headed, I'd recommend that you fold 'em and hit a fairway-finder instead. Another practical reason to work on that Tiger stinger shot.

Bill and I also talked about the benefits of pressure. In order to become a better player, you have to be able to calm the spirit and the mind and perform under pressure. Think about it: every shot comes with corresponding level of pressure. Sometimes that pressure is light, sometimes it's intense. And the source of that pressure varies widely, but it largely begins inside the mind. Bill shared a story on how his father played under pressure as often as possible: *"My father said when he was the pro at Seminole, Hogan would come down here the month before the Masters, and they played every day. But the game they played back then was: Every time you missed a fairway, you threw $10 in the hat, and every time you missed a green, you threw in $10. Well, $10 was a lot of money back then. And if you're playing that game against Ben Hogan, you better learn to play pretty quick."* Let's turn this into an exercise: Imagine putting $10 into the pot every time you missed a fairway and a green in regulation. I'm pretty confident that you'd look at the probabilities and likely modify your shot selection in order to not lose money.

Another way to become calmer under pressure is to practice under pressure as often as possible. More experience in difficult situations will certainly make you better at dealing with them. Every shot has some level of pressure attached to it, and in my experience pressure exposes weakness. Think of it as a test; increasing the water pressure through a pipe is how the hardiness of a pipe is tested. So to become a better player, practice in an environment where the pressure is heightened: play a match with a friend, and play for something of value: maybe it's a small amount of money, or maybe the loser has to do a chore, or carry the other person's bag to the car. You will quickly learn how your body responds and how you need to act to bring out your best. This lesson can't be taught: it can only be learned.

While I'm on the subjects of course management, pressure, and Ben Hogan, I want to share another Harmon quotation about Hogan. He recalled, *"When I would talk to my dad about his experiences with Ben Hogan, I don't think they talked about swing theory. He always talked about Hogan's golf course management, where to miss. My dad said Hogan had an uncanny ability to figure out what the winning score was going to be before he teed off, and then he knew how to manage that."*

Again, another instance of a great competitor doing the mental work and strategy *before* the round, to apply and stick to it *during* the round. What's remarkable to many of us, who think of Hogan as *probably* the greatest ball-striker ever, is that we learn that Hogan talked a lot about: where to miss! Talk about being completely honest with yourself, and knowing what you're capable and not capable of. What's a good habit for Hogan is a good habit for all of us.

Hogan has made a few quotations that I want to share:

- "Golf is not a game of good shots. It's a game of bad shots."
- "This is a game of misses. The guy who misses the best is going to win."
- "Placing the ball in the right position for the next shot is 80-percent of winning golf."
- "Golf is 20 percent talent and 80 percent management."

If you listen to Bill Harmon, you could be listening to Ben Hogan (just without the languid Texas drawl). Bill will certainly teach you the fundamentals of a sound swing, but he—like his brothers—is more likely to teach you how to manage yourself and the course in order to play better golf. He reminisced about a course management lesson from the master strategist, Jay Haas: "*When I started caddying for Jay, I remember... when you play the tour [event and] you tee off late Thursday, you haven't had your breakfast yet and you're eight shots back. Because someone has already shot eight-under. You haven't hit a range ball yet, and you're eight back. And we were playing somewhere and somebody had shot eight-under, and Jay bogeyed two of the first three holes. And now we're 10 shots back. And it was a par five over water and we were trying to figure out whether to go for it. As a caddie—and in my stupidity—I wanted to go, you know ... let's go [for it]. Two over! And I'll never forget, he [Haas] was about 23 or 24 years old, he said, 'Nah that is the worst thing I could do,' he said, 'I gotta lay up.*

I can still make four. I gotta get my feet on the ground.'"
Jay going through the same risk-and-reward probabilities that Faldo and Fanny would, and he realized after just making two bogeys, maybe it's not the best time to attempt a low-percentage shot. Bill drew a parallel between Jay Haas's smart decision and his father, with another quotation from his dad: *"My dad told me one time and I think this is true. 'You never gamble when you're swinging poorly; you only gamble when you're swinging well.'"* Haas also had the patience—and perspective—that he was playing a 72-hole tournament, and that he had a better chance of chasing down the leaders, though 10 shots behind already, with 69 holes to go, if he didn't make a dumb double bogey. This long-game thinking is what has helped Viktor Hovland change his perspective on a few mistakes here and there early in a tournament, and to not force hero shots to try to catch the tournament leaders. Keep steady, and let your game do the work.

Bill then shared what he referred to as Jay Haas's "magic words": *"Every stroke I save today, I don't have to make up tomorrow."* Words I believe that, if taken to heart, will unquestionably help you to better golf. If you pull off a risky shot, it may save you a stroke; put yourself in trouble, and you may lose three strokes. Think about that next time you're standing over a hero shot.

When you listen to Bill Harmon, you realize that there's so much more to good golf than having a good golf swing. And if you are wearing yourself out, banging balls on a driving range, perhaps you should take a break and listen to the Bill Harmon episode. He took me and thousands of listeners on a rollercoaster ride of moments: some somber, some that spurred introspection, some that hit us between the eyes, and some that just downright made us think.

If I could somehow summarize it all with one quotation, it would be this one from Bill: *"Gimme me tough over good, any day."*

Keep putting the work in; the scores aren't always indicative of what's going on with your game. And I always had kind of a longer-range forecast. It's really so easy to get caught in the short-term, because you got a scorecard in your pocket. You know, you've got to go post a score, either to compete with your buddies or maybe you're playing tournament golf. But to have that kind of long-range view of things is so important.

Justin Leonard

16

Justin Leonard

My Golf DNA

Justin Leonard, a 12-time PGA Tour winner, the 1997 Open Champion, the 1998 PLAYERS Champion, and a USA Ryder Cup Team hero. He may be diminutive in size, but sizable in stature with a Mensa-level golf IQ. The measured yet affable Texan always played bigger than himself, and he took down numerous giants in his lengthy professional career.

I have always looked up to Justin Leonard. From our junior golf days—Justin is two years younger than me—he was always someone who caught my eye. Given how good he was, I guess I aspired to be like him in a way. I realize now that my admiration for Justin is a function of his individuality, his golf savvy, and his incredible short game.

After his playing career, Justin spent a little time in the broadcast booth for NBC Sports. That time allowed him to share his personality—which he kept under wraps while playing—and his comprehensive insight. Leonard has a tremendous sense and feel for the game, which showed up in his announcing and analysis. He has a wonderful way of blending the science of statistics and data with the art of playing the game and creating shots, and I was intent to bring that unique mixture to our *On the Mark* chat.

The first thing that struck me, as the Justin Leonard I knew was a guy who won a lot of junior tournaments, was the fact that he was not the pick of Dallas-Fort Worth Metroplex litter. Justin remembers, *"Growing up in Dallas, I was around players that were better than me. And at Royal Oaks Country Club, when I was 13 or 14 years old, I was playing with the 15- and 16- and 17-year-olds, and they were hitting it 30 and 40 yards by me, just as some guys did once I got on the PGA Tour. So I had to find a way to compete, and I did it by a really good short game, management, managing my game, all of those things. And, while I'm sure some of those high school guys didn't enjoy having to play with a 13-year-old, I learned a lot. I learned a lot about myself and how to compete when I wasn't the strongest. I wasn't maybe the most talented, but I worked my tail off, and I loved it. For me, golf was always about putting the work in and trying to find ways to get better."* Several players included in this book learned by working very hard and playing with golfers who were older, bigger, stronger, and better than him. Justin is no exception.

No matter your age or ability, if you want to improve quickly, put your ego aside and play with golfers who are better than you. If you keep your eyes and your ears open, you'll quickly learn some tricks and tools of the trade that work for you. It reminds me of another podcast conversation I had with Dr. Ian Peek. Ian wrote his dissertation on the social psychology of high performance. After years of study and research, he discovered that high performers had two common personality traits: They spent time watching good players, and they had a habit of asking good questions.

I remember joking that when I was competing, I

was too shy and too embarrassed to ask good questions. (I certainly watched every move the good golfers made, but didn't really ask them about techniques or strategies.) The irony of it all is that now, as a podcast host and an interviewer, I ask all of the questions, on behalf of others. Sometimes I wonder what could've been, if I had done that while I was still competing ...

But I digress. Watching great players and asking good questions is a great way to learn and improve. Another way is to learn how to compete, and Justin did so by developing an immaculate short game. Remember that there are many ways to make a four. Naturally, it's easier if you hit it far, but that's not the only way to do it. A young Justin Leonard made fours, and better, by finding the fairway off the tee, getting the approach shot on or around the green, and then making a greenside save or two-putting. His is a case study in discipline, application, attitude, and course management.

Justin spoke about that approach and playing a game of precision in the power era: *"I'm not trying to hit the ball 300 yards, because it goes against my natural DNA. If I could gain five or ten yards with the driver, but not lose any accuracy—I would try, but I don't—because I'm just more comfortable hitting the ball in the fairway. I have less control than most from the rough. And so for me, it's still comfortable playing in the fairway, playing my game and not trying to emulate what the best players in the world do."* What Justin says here speaks to other ideas in this book, including knowing your game, being yourself, and owning your game.

It also begs the question, Do you know what your natural golf DNA is? I would guess that you do not. A lot of us wouldn't be able to describe our golf DNA accurately. Imagine your golf DNA as your innate abilities: mental, emotional, and physical. It also involves having an accurate assessment of your strengths and weaknesses.

The truth is that most of the amateur golfers I've given lessons to have no idea who they really are. As a result, they don't really know what they should work on, and what they should keep constant. So if golfers work on their game, it's likely that they aren't working on the right thing—or worse, trying to change something that's core to their body and ability—and so they're essentially wasting their time, and regrettably might be getting worse instead of getting better.

Let's not do that. Let's make the time count. Especially given that time is a limited commodity for most golfers, I'd advocate that you, as Justin said, "find ways to get better" by working on addressing your weaknesses and galvanizing your strengths. All the while, you need to be true to your DNA. And if you are chasing distance, be realistic about it: a distance gain of 10 to 15 yards is certainly significant, but it only becomes worthwhile if it leads to lower scores.

In later years, Justin embarked on a journey of gaining a little extra power, but he was both realistic and circumspect about it. Justin explains, *"I experiment here and there, especially with the driver swing, trying to hit a little more up on it, trying to use the ground more, because I was and I still am very much more rotational in my golf swing."* He did qualify the work though: *"I'm not gonna overhaul things to try and get better. My DNA is my DNA. My swing is my swing. But if I can add a little bit here and there along the way, I think that's what we're all trying to do."* While it's noble to attempt to add strength, agility, and distance, it's important to stay within yourself. If you get carried away, your typical, natural swing won't work the same, your timing will go awry, and things can go sideways quickly.

Speaking of Justin's golf DNA, I had to ask him about his wedge game. His wedge game was most certainly his calling card, and in my opinion, it was as good as anyone to ever play the game. He did talk about how he would do a lot of work and the emphasis was always distance, trajectory, and spin control. Justin recalled, *"In my practice, I worked on varying the heights. Basically I want to hit it as low as I can and still hit the appropriate shot, because then I'm taking spin off. You know, spin just adds another variable to it. Obviously if you're playing the U.S. Open at Bethpage Black, you have to put spin on, but day-in day-out, that's not the case. And so, controlling spin [and] trying to get the ball on the ground as quickly as possible were two things that I always thought about with my wedge play, [when] growing up and even to this day."*

In my experience, the amateur tries to go too high too often. Here is Justin Leonard, a wizard with a wedge in hand, saying that spin adds an unnecessary variable to the distance-control equation. He's not the only great wedge player to adopt that approach: I remember the great Seve Ballesteros talking about a wedge shot having just enough spin to stunt its forward progress, to allow it to roll toward the hole. Larry Mize, the architect of possibly the greatest pitch shot ever, was the same way inclined. In fact, Larry never used a wedge with more than 56 degrees of loft.

When chipping around the greens, the more time you give the ball on the ground, the more control you have over the result. As Justin said, *"get the ball on the ground as quickly as possible."* It makes sense, considering that putts from off the green are unlikely to scamper over the green, and are most likely to end closer to the hole than a lot of chip or pitch shots. That's because you have a better sense of touch and speed when the ball rolls. I'm certain that when you become comfortable with it, you'll be glad you did.

Justin also referenced creativity and shot-making in wedge play: *"If you have three wedges, just because your number falls in the parameter of your 54-degree doesn't necessarily mean it's a 54-degree [shot]. You might be better with your pitching wedge. Or maybe you're comfortable, or the green's a little firmer, then maybe you do hit your more lofted wedge hard.*" This is a learned skill, and it's worthwhile to develop, but it takes a change in the approach to practice. Leonard explains, "*In practice it's not dumping a bucket of balls and hitting one club. It's hitting to different targets. It's hitting to different numbers.*" Many elite wedge players—Justin Leonard references both Zach Johnson and Steve Stricker as models—practice to different targets and yardages on each shot during practice. Varying distance constantly—to develop feel and to dial in distance control—is a habit I see that's common on the PGA Tour. It has influenced my approach to instruction. Once one of my students has developed the requisite skill and is somewhat comfortable, I introduce them to the elements of pressure and variation. I use my FlightScope launch monitor and set up a wedge combine, which is basically a distance control test that spits out a different yardage with a different size target on each shot: just like the test that the golf course presents. It's a simple way to get instant feedback while awakening feel, in an ever-changing, pressure-filled environment. Justin Leonard is not a big user of launch monitors, but he said the activity helps with "*developing touch and an understanding of how the hands and the wedge work.*"

Taking a look at the short games of Stricker, Johnson, and Leonard, you'll see a beautiful relationship between their hands and the clubhead. That relationship involves the hands directing the clubhead with the appropriate loft through impact, the appropriate face angle through impact, and then the correct speed through impact. As you watch them hit wedges, you'll notice that there's not a lot of clubhead speed through the ball. In fact, it appears that there's a one-to-one relationship between the speed of the hands and the clubface. There is most certainly not a flash of speed through impact: rather it's smooth and timed, and the ball is not *picked,* or *dug* for that matter, but almost just *squeezed* against the turf. They all make very shallow divots, and they control the distance of the shot with height and spin. Justin describes the strike in a way that brings the shot to life. He certainly painted a picture. He called the action *"not gouge-y low, but swept off the grass low."* I love the description. Imagine what you would have to do to sweep a low wedge shot off the grass. In contrast, imagine a swing that would gouge through the turf to hit a low wedge shot. The former would deliver a flighted trajectory with the suitable amount of spin, in contrast to the latter, which would deliver an unpredictable, spinny shot that would fall to the mercy of the wind. If any golfer makes a practice swing with a wedge that bruises the turf in the proper place—just forward of center in the stance —and then tries to emulate that feeling at contact, then you're on to great form. This connects to Karl Morris's explanation of *"landing the plane"* through impact.

In my experience, those "gouge-y" swings are often the product of taking too little club and trying to over-hit a wedge. Always remember that you have an athlete inside of you, and that your brain will activate what-ever systems necessary to achieve a goal. If that goal is to get the ball to a target that's beyond your distance range with that club, your body will make pre-swing and likely mid-swing modifications to overextend. It's not a high-percentage tactic. So instead of over-powering a wedge, take one less club and swing a little easier. Here's Leonard's take: *"If it was two yards outside of my comfort zone, I would go to the next club up, and then just take some yardage off."* He believes, as do all elite players and coaches, that wedge play is a precision endeavor. Justin says it's *"more about control. It's more about understanding there's five different ways to hit a ball 87 yards with a particular club."* He's suggesting that you be creative and varied with a wedge in hand: for example, hitting a lower-flight wedge that skips forward and then spins, or a higher shot that lands and stops, or a drawing shot that lands and rolls out, and so on. So ditch the stock shot and get a little freaky and creative. You'll have fun and you will improve your wedge proximity numbers.

Don't forget: scoring clubs are about precision, with the emphasis on distance control. To be truly precise, it's about realizing there's more to the equation than just the range-finder yardage and the force and power of the swing. Justin elaborated: *"It's choosing what's best for the hole location, for the firmness of the greens, for the lie that I have, and for whatever conditions are going on above the surface, meaning wind. And it's kind of understanding and being somewhat comfortable with all five of those shots."*

For the record, as it pertains to mechanics and fundamentals, Leonard advocates that the ball position should move around in the stance to promote different trajectories. He would largely play the ball around the middle to the back-half of the stance, but he was not averse to moving the ball as far back as his back foot for a lower-flighted shot. The only time he'd move the ball forward in the stance was for a high shot that was very close to the green.

Often it looked like Leonard just caressed a wedge shot, and he never really appeared to bludgeon shots inside of 120 yards. So I quizzed Justin about how he would vary swing speed with a wedge. He responded with advice that can apply to every golfer at every skill level: *"it all starts in the grip pressure. A tight grip makes it very hard to feel your arms, and you can't control the speed. So I always played with a very light pressure, especially my wedges, and then just the practice of controlling distance. That's why, if you've got a green out there that you can practice to, start at 80 yards and hit multiple shots and hit multiple wedges. Taking speed off and getting comfortable with taking speed out of the swing and still hitting the ball and making good contact.*" The best wedge players know that so much of the shot depends on the hands: not just their position, but their pressure on the club.

To put a bow on the wedge conversation, never forget that skill with a wedge is a direct influence on the scorecard. So get out and devote some practice time to those scoring shots. And when you do, hit more wedges than drivers. You'll see a commensurate improvement in your scores, and your confidence will start to soar.

Speaking of confidence, it's paramount to any golfer's success. Justin and I talked about the delicate subject of self-belief and confidence, and how golf can knock those down in a blink of an eye. He had some thoughts on the concept: thoughts that he employed when he was competing, and thoughts that he is now teaching to his son, Luke, who also plays competitive golf. Justin shared, *"I think one of the difficult tasks is to find confidence in ways other than just the scorecard. It can't be just about what you're shooting."* Read that again and take time to mull over it. You should always remember the individual good shots, not just your overall scores. Remember that a round of golf is only comprised of golf shots, and focusing on score is a level removed from the actual play. Leonard embellished on his pre-shot decision making: *"What I try and do, in my own game is [ask myself], am I comfortable? Am I comfortable hitting a variety of shots? Because I've always moved the ball around—not big curves, but a little bit— that's how I control my distance and my height. So do I feel comfortable hitting those smaller shots, not your full stock 8-iron? But instead of it going 150, like if there's a little bit of wind, and am I comfortable hitting it 135, to a back-right hole location. You know, those kind of things."* Justin's description of his shot making and creativity got my juices flowing, and I asked him about how to practice in that mindset. His response was emphatic: *"Yeah, I think you have to practice it and find ways like that to build confidence, because [confidence] is not always going to come from the scorecard."* So in essence, confidence is built, and then galvanized, by developing different shots. By practicing skill elements like draws and fades, full shots and half shots, high shots and low shots. You build confidence by expanding your cache of weapons, increasing your dependable options to overcome a variety of situations and elements. After you have the ability to pull off these shots consistently, there won't be a shot on the course that you have not practiced, there won't be a shot you cannot hit. That should build confidence in itself. I liken it to prepping for a test. I've said that a round of golf is an exam. If you've developed and practiced all manner of shots, it's like you have prepared for every question on the test, and you have that feeling of readiness. That confidence. When you have that skill set, you *look forward* to being tested.

Confidence, however, is fickle. It's not just amateurs: Every player on the planet has lost confidence many times on the course, and that includes the very best. Justin talked about it: *"It is so fleeting. Trust me, I lost confidence plenty of times in my career. And I think I found ways to get it back by trying to do the things I do on the golf course more in my practice. Trying to hit those little shots. It wasn't just about stock numbers."* Think back to your last range session and ask yourself, How many shots did I hit that weren't my typical, full-swing speed? Did I try to hit intentionally low shots, intentionally clubbing up and swinging easy? Do I ever practice a punch shot? Pitches from tough lies? Now think about how much more confident you'd be out on the golf course if you did.

Leonard recounted a tournament example, about

not hitting just stock shots and instead being more creative, with his long-time coach, Randy Smith. (Randy has also been a guest on the *On the Mark* podcast. He's a teaching legend, who is also Scottie Scheffler's only coach, and he deserves a chapter in the next book.) Justin recalls, *"I remember a particular instance when I'd stopped working with Randy, and I was working with another instructor, and I was down in San Antonio. I hadn't been playing well for a while. And I knew Randy was going to be down there, and so I said 'Randy, could you come watch me play six holes?' This is on a Thursday and Friday, because it's very different from Wednesdays, you know, [close] to when the bell goes off."* Knowing when to ask someone to take a look at your play—not just your swing—is a pro move. Justin continued, *"So Randy came out and watched me, and then I talked to him after the round. 'I see,' he goes, 'you're trying to hit the same shot every time.' He said that's why I was lost. He said, 'go back and start creating.' He said, 'create on the range, create before the round, so that when you get on the golf course you're moving the ball around, you're creating again and hit some different shots.' So I got involved in that process. All of a sudden, the swing thoughts kind of went away. And I was simply watching the divot pattern and ball flight: as far as how does the divot look, and is the ball starting where I want to and curving the right direction. And so from then, I completely got out of the funk that I was in, because he helped me get back to playing the way I did, instead of being in the trap of just hitting one shot and playing too much golf swing."* Echoes of what Butch Harmon—and several others in this book—have said. Play golf, not golf swing. It's a story of what happens when you get a bit away from our own golfer DNA, so stay true to yourself.

It's crazy how—in the search for improvement—we can get too deep into the weeds and get away from our natural DNA. Despite our best intentions, with all of the logic and reason to back up the change ... sometimes it just doesn't work. Sometimes we've gone too far, and we need to recognize that. The good news (I guess) is that even golfers at the elite level do so. Justin continued, *"It's weird: as humans have a way to complicate things. And with all the data that's available, all the strokes-gained information, launch monitors ... it's so easy to bogged down in those things and start to over-analyze, overthink. I played the best in my career when I kept it very, very simple."* Keep it simple! The old adage— Keep It Simple, Stupid—is more often than not the best path to take. You've heard other players in this book share similar advice. Overcomplicating leads to confusion, and that confusion leads to a loss of confidence.

Simply, for lasting improvement, I advocate you cannot go wrong by focusing on basic fundamentals like aim and alignment, grip, ball position, rhythm, timing, and balance. I'm not saying focus on all of them, although that wouldn't hurt: just find the one that's holding you back from your best golf, from being true to your golfer DNA, and get it to where it should be. Learn to understand and respect your tendencies and play the game with an emphasis on nuances like course management, green reading, and a bullet-proof short game. Take ownership of your game, practice and play like Justin Leonard did and still does.

Justin shared another reason not to over-emphasize golf scores: it gets in the way of long-term improvements. He advised, *"Keep putting the work in; the scores aren't always indicative of what's going on with your game. And I always had kind of a longer-range forecast. It's really so easy to get caught in the short-term, because you got a scorecard in your pocket. You know, you've got to go post a score, either to compete with your buddies or maybe you're playing tournament golf. But to have that kind of long-range view of things is so important."* No meaningful change happens overnight; you can only get discouraged overnight. Stick with it and keep your focus on the horizon. These notions helped Justin Leonard be a giant slayer, with an incredible golf IQ and understanding of the game. Focus on what makes your game good, and stay true to what works for you while improving what doesn't. Stay engaged and creative. Practice the odd shots you have to sometimes pull off on the golf course, and you'll be ready—and confident—when it matters most. Cultivate your confidence, and have a long-view of your improvement. Justin added this about taking a longer perspective: *"I think it's just so important. Whether you're a brand-new junior golfer, college golfer, or professional, you've got to have your eye on the long run and long term when you're making decisions as far as your game and things you want to work on. You can't get so focused on the here-and-now, because the game of golf—if you do that—is going to beat you up quite a bit."*

What's the art of great teaching? It's really communication, to be able to get the message across to different people in different ways.

David Leadbetter

17

David Leadbetter

Thought Turns to Feel

David Leadbetter is like a second father to me. I feel like he's had the greatest influence on me and my career as a golf instructor. His book, *Faults and Fixes—How to Correct the 80 Most Common Problems in Golf* (1996), was one of the first game improvement books I ever purchased. I remember pouring over it, learning every concept and memorizing every drill. It was like my ABCs of Golf Teaching, and to this day I still use some of the drills Leadbetter recommended in the book.

In my opinion, "Lead"—as his friends and students call him—is the Father of Modern Golf Instruction. I stress *modern*, as gentlemen such as Percy Boomer, Ernest Jones, Harvey Penick, and John Jacobs are like the patriarchs of our industry. Everyone who came after them effectively just continued to carry the ball and develop different ways of communicating the principles of game improvement. Leadbetter led the next generation and innovated the various modes and methods of teaching.

David has a bright, inquisitive mind, and he's a master in developing training-aids to help students learn—and feel—a certain move in the swing or the stroke. He has a paternal nature about him, and he's forever patient: these two traits contribute to his success as a teacher of all skill levels.

In our podcast recording, David's amiable personality is clearly evident. He makes complicated golf technique concepts appear simple, and he always elaborates on them with a story or a recollection from his work with legends of the game such Nick Faldo, Nick Price, and Ernie Els. Despite his legendary stature, he's still very humble. When I asked David about being a leading teacher, he declined the spotlight and spoke about the traits required to mentor and teach: *"Look, the thing is ... What's the art of great teaching? It's really communication, to be able to get the message across to different people in different ways."*

For posterity's sake, he did venture further, given the approaches to golf instruction today. David has the perspective that only comes from teaching through several eras—and many trends and fads—to see what are the basic essentials, and what are tools for those teaching essentials. He discussed the role of technology over the past 30 years: *"Technology is wonderful, but it's only a tool; video is wonderful, but it's only a tool. You can overuse these things to the point where you can actually make somebody more technical. I mean, sports psychologists hate all that stuff, because the fact is, they're trying to clear people's minds, not clutter them."*

This is coming from a guy who was often criticized for being too technical. In fact, I thought David was very technical before I met him. How wrong I was! The truth is that David will employ whatever it takes to help a student to understand and implement an improvement. Indeed it was through David Leadbetter that I met sports psychologist Dr. Bob Winters, whom David employed as the lead sports psychologist at his Leadbetter Academy Global Headquarters.

Lead exhibited his all-encompassing teaching nature when he shared an anecdote from his extensive work with Nick Faldo: *"One of the things that we did a lot when I was out with Nick: he'd like a couple of technical thoughts, but I always used to put them in a feel mode, so everything would be done in pairs. So for instance, if we were trying to say, 'keep a little more flex in your right knee, and I want you to move your left shoulder away from your chin as you start down.' So we would say 'okay, sit and pull, sit and pull,' and you'd hear him mouthing these words. 'Sit and pull; sit and pull.'"*

It's important to understand the theories behind a change, but they often get in the way of actually implementing them: many golfers—even pros—can make a change more effectively when they can translate it into a feeling in the body. David continued: *"So that was really my job at tournaments: to actually find the keyword that actually enabled him [Faldo] to have that rhythm, which was sort of like, 'back and through, up and down,' ... whatever it may be, you know, something on those lines."* Isn't it cool how—when teaching something complicated and technical—David boils the idea down into just a few words and a feel?

I love that for various learning reasons. First, improvement happens, as Bobby Jones used to say, "when a golfer has the fewest things to think about." Secondly, swing thoughts should elicit a positive response, and they should be simple and actionable and reproducible. Third, I believe the that the majority of golfers and lesson-takers lose a lot of information in translation. After every lesson I give, every lesson, I ask the learner what they learned. I can honestly say that every golfer recalls only a portion of the lesson and what they learned. This is just human nature. Consider the children's game Telephone, also known as Chinese Whispers—no matter how much care is taken in retelling the message to the next person in line, errors always accumulate as the message makes its way along the chain.

So, the lesson—for all you lesson-takers—is to ensure you distill all the information received into something that is understandable, digestible, and most importantly: memorable. Nick Faldo always made sure he did, and it worked out pretty well for him.

Speaking of the six-time major champion and hall-of-famer, I asked Leadbetter about his work with Faldo, when they resolved to rebuild Sir Nick's swing to empower him to be able to control his trajectory more effectively in the wind. In a nutshell, David and Nick eliminated excess leg action while changing the swing from a more up and down action to a more rounded movement. David recalls that Faldo *"was an amazing technician. Especially with his irons, being able to control distance and trajectory and shape, and so really it worked out well. He was just the perfect student. No two ways about it. He was the perfect student. He worked really hard, and he was bound and determined to get it. We both were working towards the same end, and there was no thought that he was not going to get it."*

Improvement requires work: it's as simple as that. The ugly truth is that you could take a lesson from the Messiah, but if you don't work on it and groove it, there's little chance it will settle and turn into improvement. Leadbetter described Faldo as the perfect student, and said that Sir Nick worked really hard and was determined to get it. This speaks to the mindset of learners who get it and who succeed. In my experience, it's always been the focused, hard workers who were the ones who have succeeded in making swing changes, game improvement changes, and adjustments. Successful folks go all in. There are no half-measures, nothing is left to chance. And if you want to make changes that last, a Faldo-like approach and attitude is all but mandatory. It wasn't just Nick's manner that played a major part in his development from good to great. Check out the uncanny power of his mind in achieving the timeline for change that Leadbetter predicted: *"it was interesting how I told him [Faldo] … I just sort of took a wild guess at it in some respects. I said, 'listen it's probably going to take us a couple of years before you feel totally comfortable.' And it was amazing there, Mark, it was only literally just past a couple of years when won his first Open at Muirfield."*

David continued to elaborate on Faldo's work methods and, in my mind, taught my podcast-listeners how to turn technical work into on-course improvements. He explained, *"there has to be some thought, and thought needs to turn into feel. And so ultimately, that's what Nick was able to do. And he was very far from being a technical player. He was a technical player to the point where he liked the technique. He knew where it had to be, but you get him on the golf course. I mean, it was amazing Mark, I could not tell you what his strongest sensory system was because, he was always whistling, he was clicking. He could visualize things, he could feel things, you know: his visual, his kinesthetic, his audio. It was amazing: he had all the systems working."*

In other words, Faldo employed most of his senses when he was on course. It wasn't just the feel of technique. Leadbetter continued: *"And so he would just hit shots. I mean, even when we were practicing, it wouldn't just be pure technique; and even my good friend, Nick Price, did the same thing. The thing is, what people need to learn—especially youngsters—is that when you're out there practicing, and you're working on it, you want to throw in a lot of shots like you're on the golf course. You don't want to stand on a tee, like a robot, because that's not really how you're playing golf.*" Another key takeaway: practice like you play, and it'll be the most beneficial practice session possible.

Think about a round of golf. When do you get an exact yardage, how often do you have a perfectly level lie? How often do you have a good lie? You need to be prepared for all of these eventualities. I remember the Benjamin Franklin quotation: "Failing to prepare is preparing to fail."

Now, with the benefit of hindsight and experience, I can categorically say that when I competed, I had the whole thing backward. I thought—incorrectly—that the more I worked on my swing, the more my scores would improve. Now if my swing was better, I'd probably strike that ball a little more consistently and a little more solidly, but that never, ever translated into lower scores.

The Nicks—Faldo and Price—probably Leadbetter's most decorated students—had it right. Productive practice involves some technical work to develop the change, but then it should pivot to shot making and creation. How I wish I had done that when I was coming up!

Anyway, here we are. Now as a teacher of aspiring golfers, I also advise that students practice shots from different lies, especially around the greens. If you go to a PGA Tour event, you'll see the game's best continually practice from the rough, the sand, basically everywhere to learn how the club and the ball react as they prepare for the tournament conditions. To use Lead's term *robots*, the pros aren't robots just hitting autopilot 7-irons. They're professionals who—through creativity and skill—manufacture shots, so that they can make birdies and save pars.

Being the golf swing junkie that I am, I had to ask David about his beliefs on the golf swing. He quipped, *"I know it's still a mystery, I can tell you that."* Then he got serious and launched into a simple but profound description of his beliefs on how an efficient swing functions: *"I've always believed there's three components in the golf swing. One is your set up: the grip, posture, and alignment: the foundational stuff in the swing. The second component is your body movement: how your trunk moves, how your hips, your core, your shoulders, how they move, wind, rotate, move forward, and then re-rotate. And then the third component would be the hand, arm, and club components. So you've got three components which have to sort of synchronize. Once you've got the setup, then the synchronization—for the most part—happens between your torso and your arms and how those two blend together. [That blending], to me, is the key for a good swing. When you feel that your timing is good, your rhythm is good ... to me, it's all about synchronization.*

As it pertains to the golf swing, synchronization of moving parts—or more simply, timing—is as misunderstood and disrespected as any element. And trust me, I have seen some technically sound swings completely misfire due to bad timing and poor synchronization.

To me, a golf swing is like an orchestra. Obviously, the orchestra is a collection of musicians, each playing their own instrument with their own role. When they all play in time, and at the correct time, they produce a stirring symphony. However, if just one person plays out of time—or comes in at the incorrect time—the whole thing turns into a cacophony. There is discord, and then every other musician is thrown off their timing in an effort to re-establish musical order. The orchestra must rely on their own practice, and the conductor, to keep everything in time.

The golf swing operates in the same fashion. Every functional element of the swing could be operating appropriately, but if they are firing at the wrong time in relation to each other, then dissonance sets in and results are compromised.

Thinking of the golf swing in three distinct

components—like Leadbetter does—makes the timing and coordination of their movement a little easier. Not that organizing timing is ever easy: it is achievable and it should be practiced; and it certainly should be respected as a reason for miss-hit and faulty golf shots. Lead continued further and explained how faulty sequencing can come in various forms: *"to me, it's all about synchronization. To me, you find players, good players in particular, whose bodies run away, and the arms can't catch up, and they're stuck. And we see with poor players where the arms, shoulders start down and the lower body doesn't work. There's a disparity between the body parts and the swing itself."*

Leadbetter elaborated on how well-timed players tend to have a backswing where the shaft plane is a little steeper, and that allows the downswing shaft plane to shallow. This move—which he endorsed with his approach to his A-Swing (alternative swing) concept—makes coordination and timing of the moving parts a little easier, thanks to a simpler backswing. While doing that, he made a statement that resonated with me: *"Most people get so stuck and hung up on the backswing they never make the downswing, or they never have any downswing thoughts."*

I completely agree with David that the downswing is infinitely more important than the backswing, because you hit the ball with your downswing. I'll counter though that the backswing is about 75% of the golf swing, and a sound backswing does set up a decent downswing.

I've seen many good golfers with funky-looking backswings, so an off-kilter backswing won't limit success. If, however, you're focusing on your backswing, focus mostly on the clubface orientation at the top, and the quality and location of the body's pivot, which are related to the shift of pressure in the feet.

I quizzed Lead on his thoughts on the modern-day

proliferation of shut clubfaces at the top of the swing. For what it's worth, I prefer a more neutral face alignment at the top of the swing as that affords the golfer the luxury of using forearm rotation and wrist unhinging alignments to square the face through contact. I like this open-to-shut mechanism—which is like a door slamming shut—as it facilitates a little extra clubhead speed through impact. And we could all use a little of that!

Before he shared his perspective on the shut clubface at the top, he explained how trends and flavor-of-the-moment swings or techniques come and go, but not without unintentionally ruining a few good golfers and swings all the way. David said, *"We always see, when you get some great player, great ball-striker, they tend to be sort of the flavor [of the time], don't they? And everybody says 'okay this is what we need to do.'"* It's a syndrome that is rampant on the PGA Tour and definitely evident at golf courses around the world. I'm not saying that you shouldn't emulate leading players to a point, but I'm saying that succumbing hook, line, and sinker to this syndrome can be a dangerous endeavor.

You've probably seen, heard, and read about these trends or swings that have had a great influence over swing changes. But hopefully you've also seen, heard, and read about how many top-flight instructors and top-level players have kept to what works and what works for a particular person, rather than applying one person's swing to another's. In other words, just because your friend is using a new driver shaft that has gained him some distance, it doesn't mean that you should use the same one. Or just because your friend is working on a certain area of his swing, and he's getting better, that doesn't mean you should try the same focus or swing move.

Out on the PGA Tour, too many players are always looking over their shoulders to see what the guys who are playing well are doing. Leadbetter referenced

Dustin Johnson and Daniel Berger who play with closed clubfaces at the top, but they both have a strong body move to align the clubface appropriately at impact. Not everybody can do this consistently, either because of a lack of mobility or strength, or because of a lack of practice and/or practice time! It's as simple as that.

David emphasized a more natural approach that's in tune with one's own body, and how the pieces of the swing work together for you. He said, *"To me, there's a natural way of swinging the golf club, and it's interesting to me how our good friend, Gary Player ... you speak to him and you ask him what his thoughts would be, if he could change his philosophy over the years, it would be to get the face or open [or] hanging at the top of the backswing. And that's essentially what Ben Hogan did to cure his hook. And we know modern players are very strong. I mean, their core: they're amazingly strong. They're pullers of the golf club. They hang on to it, and it's interesting to see how that's going to last."* As club and ball technology has advanced, it's afforded—and also mandated—new ways of swinging. Players can rotate faster and swing harder with more forgiving clubhead shapes, bigger clubfaces, and lighter shafts that have more specific features. A great swing with today's drivers isn't the same as a swing that would work with a small persimmon head and basic steel shaft.

Related to the aggressive swings of today's younger tour pros, Leadbetter also emphasized the importance of a swing that can work over years and years: a swing that won't lead to physical problems down the road. Referring to the pros who swing an aggressive way, with body positions that are difficult to replicate, David joked, *"Maybe these guys make so much money that they don't have to play any more. From a longevity standpoint, you look at a player like a Hale Irwin, or something that has gone on for years and years; look how long Jack Nicklaus's swing has lasted. You look at a Freddie*

Couples, those sorts of players." David's making a point not only about club position and body movement, but about the longevity of some swing types over others. In my opinion, most amateurs don't have the strength, speed, and mobility to pull the club through impact and still get sufficient distance. On the other side of the coin is the fact that a pulling of the handle to keep the clubface from closing too much sacrifices the ability to crack the whip: sling the clubface through impact and gather extra clubhead speed. Imagine that golfer who can hit the ball a long way despite looking like they are barely exerting themselves: smooth swingers like Sam Snead, Fred Couples, Ernie Els, and Louis Oosthuizen spring to mind.

I break types of golf swings down into two buckets: Swingers and Hitters. A Swinger's swing is characterized by a freer swing of the clubhead supported by the movement of the body—typically the body movement and pivot are quieter and less violent. A Hitter's swing has a more energetic, fast, and vigorous body movement that governs the movement of the club a lot more. The Swinger action plays more open-to-closed with the clubface, while the Hitter hits with a clubface that operates in a closed-to-open fashion. When I try to help a higher-handicapped golfer improve their shots, I always start with the clubface, because it is the only way to influence change in the passage of the golf ball. And I'm always trying to move from the extremes to the middle of the spectrum. For example:

- Too closed a clubface becoming a hair more open. Too open of a clubface closing down a little more.

- Too violent a body-action becoming more sedate and too lazy a body-action becoming more athletic.

In the final analysis, the golf ball should travel more efficiently and accurately once the adjustment has been made. That is the acid test for every swing change!

And to be clear, if the ball isn't traveling any better, then either the lesson-taker isn't doing what is required, or not doing it enough ... or maybe the adjustment is just not the correct one for them.

I cannot stress this enough. The golf ball does not have a brain: It cannot make decisions for you, and it only does what your clubface tells it. Therefore, if the clubface is preforming better—in terms of alignment, path, angle of attack, and speed—the ball will oblige with heartening results.

Leadbetter continued sharing his insights on the golf swing and varying clubface orientations at the top of the swing as he offered advice to golf teachers: *"I have seen some players, and I have got a couple of players to get a little stronger [closed face] and pull a little more, because they might be a little 'flippy,' but yeah, once again, that's where as a teacher, you got to look at the student, and you've got to figure out what's going to help this particular player. You can't mold everybody with the same action. I mean, so many players—let's face it—have grown up with certain actions, and I think they'd be successful as long as they don't tinker. I mean, if you look at Jordan Spieth, for instance, he has a weak grip; he's got a little bowed left wrist, the left elbow buckles; the left knee collapses a little bit, but you know, he's made that work. He's hit thousands upon thousands of shots, and he makes it work. And he's a brilliant putter. And you can't say well, listen, you got to change all of that. Then again, he's not necessarily the model either."*

It's at this juncture that I'll admit that as a young instructor, I used the same models for every golf lesson I gave. Thankfully, back then I basically only focused on fundamentals and clubface performance, so I didn't do too much damage. But I guess that if I did encounter a Jordan Spieth-like example, it may have flummoxed me, and I would have proceeded on a wing and a prayer. Now, with the benefit of hindsight, some wisdom, and a lot of time spent with great minds of the game, I can most assuredly say that there is no one way of doing golf, and that golf instruction must act accordingly. The only hard line is that the object of the game is to get the ball into the hole in as few strokes as possible. So know thyself and be true to thyself.

And do not be afraid to go on a journey of knowledge and information accumulation as you work toward achieving your goals. Dig into it. Or as David Leadbetter has said to me, *"I need something to chew on."* Chew on everything. Experience it with all of your sensibilities. Work hard, but have fun. The future is yours.

18

A FINAL WORD

Mark Immelman

One day, when I pass on to the perfectly manicured fairways of heaven, I'd love my ashes to be spread on one or two golf courses, as well as on a driving range somewhere. On that range, I'd appreciate the smallest of plaques to commemorate what has been the most blessed time in golf. That plaque must read: *"To Mark, a man who loved golf, and a Coach who taught Bad Golfers to hook the ball and Good Golfers not to hook the ball."*

The reason for this inscription is that I've realized that golf is as simple as that. It is a game of spin. And one can fix hooks with slices and slices with hooks.

Golf is also a game of recovery. Every shot struck is defined by the shot that follows it. Sometimes—okay, often—that wretched golf ball finds some nasty spots. And the elite golfer—certainly the consistent scorer—is able to extricate themselves from those predicaments with limited damage to the scorecard.

At its root, golf is very simple. To channel Butch Harmon's insights: golf is certainly not easy, but it's simple ... if you can grasp those two simple concepts.

It'd be intellectually lazy of me, however, not to recognize that golf is indeed a mental and an emotional game. It is, as Bobby Jones once said, a game "played mainly on a five-and-a-half-inch course: the space between your ears."

It's for that very reason that I always gravitate toward a holistic tack when I seek out guests and topics for my *On the Mark* podcast. I've sought out a wide range of perspectives and styles—both of tour pros and teaching pros—to identify the commonalities that they share, and how their different approaches can help the different swings out there. The podcast is a labor of love for me, and I'm immensely proud of what it has become, and for the number of golfers around the world it has helped.

For those of you that have listened with any amount of frequency, you'll certainly have heard me preach about knowledge, wisdom, and understanding. We are fortunate to be in an era when the knowledge base seems to be expanding by the day. The internet is a treasure trove of insights and information, and I advocate that you constantly be in a place of seeking that out and learning. That is, expanding your knowledge. Always be learning, in golf and in life.

It doesn't end there, though. Being wise in what you choose to work on—and the best way how—takes a healthy heap of understanding. That means understanding the topic well enough to decide if it's applicable to you and your circumstance, and if so, how much of the insight you need to pursue.

My podcast's mission is to introduce the knowledge to you, but my personal goal is to navigate the conversations and lead the interview so that you, our listeners, leave the chat with that "aha" moment. That moment where it makes sense. That moment where you understand the concept enough to move it from a cerebral sense to a feel, or something tangible that is easily undertaken and applied in practice and on the course.

I leave you with this parting shot. It essentially represents my holistic beliefs, accumulated over years and at every level in golf. It's a watchword of sorts, that if respected and adhered to, is guaranteed to guide you to your golfing promised land.

It is, in a word, *On the Mark.*

O—Onto the Next, Always—The next shot is the one that defines the current shot. The next day brings hope anew. When the shot or the day is done, don't belabor it. Learn from it and then look forward.

N—Never Mind the Rest—Focus on yourself. Don't get wrapped up in other peoples' business, and certainly don't concern yourself with their thoughts and opinions of you.

T—The Clubface Matters—Be aware of its orientation at all times. It's your sole means of communication with the golf ball—and the golf ball's performance affects your reputation as a golfer.

H—Humility over Arrogance—In every aspect of the game, and in life, humility always wins over. And as it relates to golf, a humble assessment of your skill set is crucial to smart decision making.

E—Expect a Little, Strive for a Lot—Expectations are score-ruiners. Just keep doing your best.

M—Manage Your Decision Making—Golf at its essence is a game of probability and fortune, and your attitude should remove emotion from the decision making process.

A—Ask Pointed Questions—Everything happens for a reason, and as a result, everything you try should have a valid reason for its employment, and you should have a thorough understanding of the concept. Remember, you're the one with your hands on the rubber end of the golf club. The proverbial buck stops with you.

R—Resilience and Recovery—Every great player handles ups and downs, and golf is riddled with ups and downs, ebbs and flows and positive and negative events. The one who consistently recovers is the one who remains steadfast to the task at hand and the one who personifies one of my favorite phrases: "Winners find a way."

K—Kill the Auto-Pilot—Play and practice with focus and intent, at *all* times. Every shot has a value. That value is "1." So whether it is a 2-foot putt or a 300-yard drive, it's worth the same value on the scorecard. By definition, therefore, every shot deserves the same amount of application and attention. Don't short-change yourself, in practice or in play, by hitting a shot on auto-pilot (basically without your utmost attention).

With much love, devotion, and gratitude.
/mi

ACKNOWLEDGMENTS

Exodus 4:10-12

I am a blessed man, and I have been fortunate that many people have been prepared to pour into me, spiritually, mentally, emotionally, and physically.

I am the man that I am given the investment of those people. Indeed, this book is as much a part of them as it is a work of mine.

I am eternally grateful to Jesus Christ my Lord and Savior, my mother, June and my father, Johan, and my wife Tracy and girls, Isabel, and Sophia, for their selfless love and sacrifice for me.

I am also thankful to Kyle Jackson and Michelle Greef, and Trevor Immelman for their love and prayers.

The folks over at the PGA TOUR, who made my podcast a reality, deserve acknowledgement. Greg Hopfe, Dave Logue, Jason Boddy, and Chris Sinclair: Thank you for taking a chance on the *On the Mark* podcast and supporting me along the way. Who knew it was going to turn into the global juggernaut is has become.

To all of the PGA TOUR players, golf instructors, coaches, trainers, psychologists, and other bright minds who have graced me with their time and insights, Thank you! This show would not have been possible without you.

Finally, to the loyal *On the Mark* fans, thank you for trusting me as a source for game improvement information and insight. Your support and your downloads have added credence and viability to my podcast. Not in my wildest dreams did I ever fathom my little show would garner the support of millions around the globe. Again, thank you! Each and every download of yours has added to a dream come true for me.

May God bless each and every one of you richly.

INDEX

ABOUT THE AUTHOR

Mark Immelman is a teaching professional, TV golf commentator and analyst, popular podcaster, and former college golf coach. You've heard Mark provide his expert perspective on CBS, the NBC Golf Channel, ESPN+, PGA Tour Live, and Sirius XM PGA TOUR Radio. He's also worked as an analyst for many years at The Masters, the PGA Championship, and the Presidents Cup. His podcast, *On the Mark*, has received over 7 million downloads in more than 125 countries.

He earned high honors in college golf, playing on two national championship teams at Columbus State University, where he was named an All-American. Years later, as the coach of that same team, he was named 2009 NCAA Division II Coach of the Year. In 2019, he was honored to coach and captain the International team at the prestigious Arnold Palmer Cup, leading his team to victory.

Mark's knowledge, insight and experience have made him a sought-after mind on the PGA and European tours. Through his career, he has taught and/or consulted to various major champions, PGA Tour winners and global Tour professionals such as: Louis Oosthuizen, Charl Schwartzel, Patton Kizzire, Larry Mize, Loren Roberts, and yes: his younger brother, Masters champion Trevor Immelman.

Born and bred in South Africa, Immelman is now an American citizen who lives in Georgia with his wife and two daughters.